WOLVES

WOLVES

Kit Coppard

GREENWICH EDITIONS

This edition published 1999 by
PRC Publishing Ltd,
Kiln House, 210 New Kings Road, London SW6 4NZ

Produced for Greenwich Editions
10, Blenheim Court, Brewery Road
London, N7 9NT

ISBN 0 86288 297 4

Printed and bound in China

Contents

INTRODUCTION

The wolf's closest relative is the domestic dog. It is ironic that, while Western man insists that the dog is his best friend, he has long regarded the wolf with an intense but largely irrational fear and loathing, ascribing to it the murderous instincts to which only man himself can lay claim. This fear has roots in ancient religions in which the wolf is associated with death rituals. And it has inspired many myths and folk tales — we all know what happened to Little Red Riding Hood's granny. Yet the wolf and its close relatives are fascinating animals — intelligent, resourceful, and capable of surviving in a remarkably wide range of environments in spite of being hunted relentlessly wherever human settlement has impinged on their territories.

The most distant ancestors of the wolf can be traced in the fossil record back about 50 million years to a family of mammals known as the Miacidae. The miacids were small, mainly arboreal creatures somewhat resembling a present-day weasel. At about this time, in the early part of the Eocene epoch (which lasted from about 55 million to about 38 million years ago), there was a shift in the Earth's climate that was to have radical consequences for every form of plant and animal life.

Over a period of some 20 million years the planet became significantly cooler and drier, with the result that many of the tropical forests that had covered vast tracts of the land surface began to give way, first to more open woodland and later to savanna, plains, and steppes. Later still, glaciation of vast regions of the Northern Hemisphere led to a considerable drop in sea level all over the world and to the formation of "land-bridges" that joined regions and continents that formerly had been separated by seas.

With the gradual disappearance of their forest habitat, the miacids and other mammals equally gradually adapted to the necessities, perils, and advantages of ground-dwelling existence. The miacids, for instance, not only grew in size but evolved into creodonts. The term means "flesh-teeth" and refers to the teeth, known as carnassials, that are found in all the carnivorous mammals. Animals that belong to the order

WOLVES

Carnivora ("meat-eaters") begin to appear in the fossil record in the middle of the Eocene epoch, about 45 million years ago. Wolves belong to the family known as the Canidae, which also includes the domestic dog, foxes, and a number of other related, more or less wolf-like animals. The other families of the terrestrial Carnivora are the bears (Ursidae), hyenas (Hyaenidae), cats (Felidae), raccoons (Procyonidae), weasels (Mustelidae), and civets (Viverridae).

The ancestors of the canids seem to have arisen in North America, where fossil remnants dating to the end of the Eocene have been discovered. Among the earliest of these ancestors was the mongoose-like *Hesperocyon*. Short-legged and no more than 28–30in (72–76cm) long, *Hesperocyon* bore scant resemblance to present-day canids; but it had certain significant physiological features that are common to almost all the modern members of the Canidae family. For instance, its total of 42 teeth consisted of 20 in the upper jaw

Above: A pair of cape fox cubs (*Vulpes chama*). This wild canid is widespread in Africa south of the Zambesi river. Also known as the silver jackal and kama fox, it is hunted relentlessly by farmers.

Left: A gray wolf (*Canis lupus*) and six-week-old cub. Most adult members of a wolf pack help to look after the cubs.

Pages 6–7: In pursuit of prey, a gray wolf runs effortlessly through deep snow.

(where the last molar on each side was absent) and 22 in the lower. Moreover, the dentition followed the carnivore's arrangement of carnassial teeth (the first molar on each side of the lower jaw and the last premolar on each side of the upper jaw), which enable the shearing action necessary to slice through flesh.

Another significant evolutionary development concerned the dome-like protrusions known as the auditory bullae, which are located at the base of the skull just behind the lower-jaw sockets. Each bulla consists of a chamber that houses the bones of the middle ear, which connects the

Above: Pale-colored gray wolves are commonest in the tundra and arctic regions.

Right: Darker markings are more often found farther south: this timber wolf is crossing a river in Crazy Mountains, Montana.

eardrum to the inner ear and so transmits sound signals to the brain. In some mammals the bullae are made of cartilage, whereas in *Hesperocyon* (as in all true carnivores) they had become ossified into bone.

A third feature concerns the way *Hesperocyon* moved. Like the canids (and like the cats, among others), it walked and ran with a digitigrade action — that is, on its toes — whereas bears (and man) have a plantigrade action, in which the whole foot, including the calcaneus (heel), is placed on the ground.

Some 38 million years ago a split in the main evolutionary stem of the Carnivora gave rise to the ancestors of the bears and also to a mainly Eurasian group known as amphicyonids, or half-dogs. During the later Oligocene, 28–30 million years ago, the amphicyonids entered North America via the land-bridge that had developed across the Bering Strait (which divides present-day Alaska from the easternmost tip of Siberia) in the course of extensive glaciation of northern Eurasia and North America.

At about the same time, other canids similar to *Hesperocyon* arose in North America and, migrating in the opposite direction, crossed the land-bridge into Siberia and eventually colonized much of Eurasia. At the close of the Oligocene epoch, some 25 million years ago, hesperocyonic dogs became extinct and were replaced by the amphicyonids until the latter, too, died out in the late Miocene, about eight million years ago.

One of the earliest canids whose fossils display unmistakably wolf-like features was *Cynodesmus*. Its fossils were first discovered in Nebraska and date from the close of the Oligocene, about 25 million years ago. *Cynodesmus* somewhat resembled a small wolf, with relatively long legs and tail; but the first toe on each foot — which would become the dew claw in later canids — was still in contact with the ground. Even more wolf-like was the slightly later *Tomarctus*, in which the first toe was vestigial on the hind feet and greatly reduced on the fore feet. *Tomarctus*, which appeared in the early Miocene, some 20 million years ago, was ancestral to both wolves and foxes, whose forerunners begin to display clear evolutionary separation in fossils from the middle of the Miocene, about five million years later.

THE COMING OF THE WOLF

Between 7.5 and 5 million years ago the first true wolf-dogs crossed the Bering land-bridge from North America into Asia. These were small canids, probably about the size of a modern fox, highly opportunistic by necessity, scavengers as much as hunters, omnivorous in diet, and for meat relying as much on carrion as on the small animals they were capable of hunting down and killing. Their generalized feeding habits enabled them gradually to spread throughout much of the Old World and the New: in Eurasia they gave rise to the ancestors of the jackals; in North America to the forerunners of the coyote.

At this time the Earth's climate had become colder and drier again, and over vast stretches of the Northern Hemisphere forests and woodlands had given way to grassland and steppe. During this period a very diverse and extensive population of carnivores and their prey evolved in Eurasia and North America. In some regions, many of the larger, slow-moving herbivores, such as mammoths, were gradually giving way to fleet-footed ungulates such as antelopes. Some of the canids, notably the wolves, that would be among the main predators of the larger ungulates, perforce evolved into larger and speedier animals.

By the early Pleistocene epoch, about 1.5 million years ago, canids had spread westwards right across Asia and into Europe: several species of wolf as well as the dhole, or Asiatic wild dog (*Cuon*), the raccoon dog, and many species of Old World foxes (*Vulpes*) appear in the fossil record from this epoch. At about the same time, foxes spread into Africa via the Middle East, some adapting successfully to life in the Sahara and other deserts that had gradually spread over an increasing area from about four million years ago.

The Pleistocene epoch, which began about two million years ago, was characterized by a series of climatic oscillations in which episodes of glaciation (the so-called ice ages) were interspersed with interglacial episodes averaging about 10,000 years. The epoch concluded with the ending of the last ice age, about 10,000 years ago. (The present epoch is called the Holocene or, more simply, Recent.) At the peak of the most recent glaciation, some 18,000 years ago, about one twentieth of Earth's atmospheric and sea water was locked up in ice-caps, and sea levels dropped by as much as 330ft (100m) — whence the emergence of the land-bridges from the floors of what had once been, and would later revert to, shallow seas. In addition to the one across Bering Strait, an important land-bridge occupying most of what is now the North Sea linked the British Isles to Europe; another linked western Indonesia to Asia; a third joined New Guinea and Australia; a fourth connected south-western Europe to North Africa across the Strait of Gibraltar. All of these played a part in the migration of animals between the continents.

Right: Jackals, which today are confined almost exclusively to Africa, and their North American cousin the coyote evolved from a common Eurasian ancestor some two million years ago. This black-backed jackal (*Canis mesomelas*) is on the lookout for prey in Kenya's Masai Mara Game Reserve.

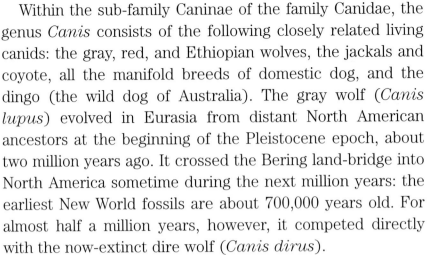

Within the sub-family Caninae of the family Canidae, the genus *Canis* consists of the following closely related living canids: the gray, red, and Ethiopian wolves, the jackals and coyote, all the manifold breeds of domestic dog, and the dingo (the wild dog of Australia). The gray wolf (*Canis lupus*) evolved in Eurasia from distant North American ancestors at the beginning of the Pleistocene epoch, about two million years ago. It crossed the Bering land-bridge into North America sometime during the next million years: the earliest New World fossils are about 700,000 years old. For almost half a million years, however, it competed directly with the now-extinct dire wolf (*Canis dirus*).

The dire wolf's origins are at least as old as that of the gray wolf, but it evolved in, and remained solely an inhabitant of, the New World where, until it passed into extinction 7,500 to 8,000 years ago, it was more widespread and for long more numerous than its gray cousin: unlike the gray wolf, it colonized large areas of South America. The largest dire wolves seem to have been even bigger than the largest gray wolves — more than 6ft 6in (2m) long from nose to tip of tail — of a somewhat heavier build, and with slightly shorter but more massive limbs than the modern gray wolf. Its head was larger and broader, and it had larger teeth. It was almost certainly less fleet-footed than the gray and perhaps also lacked the extraordinary stamina that enables the latter to pursue large, fast-moving ungulates for miles. It may have been these factors that led to its extinction.

Some two million years ago, even before the gray wolf had crossed the Bering land-bridge into North America, another Eurasian canid, the hare-eating coyote (*Canis leptophagus*), had made the journey to the New World; it evolved into the modern coyote (*C. latrans*), which today is found only in North America. Meanwhile, some of the ancestral coyotes

Above Left: The gray wolf evolved in Eurasia from distant North American ancestors and spread throughout the Holarctic region.

Left: The red fox (*Vulpes vulpes*) has by far the largest range of any wild canid: it is found throughout most of Eurasia and parts of North Africa, as well as in the United States, Canada, and Australia.

Above Right: A slightly smaller subspecies of the gray wolf, the Mexican wolf (*Canis lupus baileyi*) is in extreme danger of extinction in the wild.

Right: The husky is one of the many hundreds of breeds of domestic dogs (all classified as *Canis familiaris*) descended from the gray wolf. Arctic peoples mate huskies with gray wolves to refresh the bloodlines of the working dogs.

that remained in Eurasia spread south and west from Siberia, eventually giving rise to the golden jackal (*C. aureus*) of southwestern Asia, northern Africa, and the Balkans; and to two species nowadays found only in Africa — the side-striped jackal (*C. adustus*) and the black-backed jackal (*C. mesomelas*).

In North America the gray wolf, by now hunting in packs, filled the dire wolf's niche and its territory, and, in the process of becoming a dominant predator, it drove the coyote into more arid lands farther south and west. In Eurasia, as in North America, there was abundant food for the wolf as the Holarctic emerged from the effects of the last ice age. In the far north of its range, where the retreating glaciers left tundra in their wake, musk-ox and caribou (wild reindeer) became important items of prey. Farther south, where the damp evergreen forests of the taiga gave way to grasslands and steppe, vast herds of moose, elk, deer and other ungulates roamed over the regions formerly home to the larger herbivores that had passed into extinction. Today, although it ranges over almost as great an area of the Northern Hemisphere as the red fox, the gray wolf has largely disappeared from the United States and most of western Europe. And although it still exists in large numbers in parts of Canada, Alaska and much of northern Russia and central and eastern Asia, it has for 200 years been slaughtered on a massive scale in almost every habitat where stock-farming impinges on its age-old hunting grounds.

All the 350 or so modern breeds of dogs belong to the species *Canis familiaris*. And, together with the husky, malamute and other working dogs bred by peoples native to the Holarctic in Eurasia and North America, they all descend from the gray wolf. Indeed, even today, blood lines of the Holarctic working dogs are being refreshed by mating them with gray wolves, which will also breed with feral (that is, escaped domestic) dogs. The domestication of the dog began some 12,000 to 15,000 years ago — perhaps starting with tribesmen adopting orphaned wolf cubs, which later bred but remained with the tribe after becoming habituated to, and to some degree dependent on, human society. Archaeological finds in the United States and elsewhere suggest that selective breeding of dogs began soon after domestication got under way. Interestingly, the most wolf-like breeds are not necessarily the oldest: the dog that most closely resembles

the wolf in general appearance — the German shepherd, or Alsatian, which was deliberately bred to resemble the gray wolf — dates only from the 19th century.

Australia's only canid, the dingo, is classified as a sub-species of the domestic dog: *Canis familiaris dingo*. It was brought to the continent by Aborigines between 8,000 and 4,000 years ago, but it has never been used by them as a working dog. It is clearly a descendant of the wolf, although the exact line of its evolutionary pathway is still not known.

Within the genus *Canis* the gray wolf and the domestic dog are closest kin. The coyote and jackals, tracing their immediate common descent some two million years ago from the Eurasian hare-eating coyote, are less closely related to the wolf. It is believed that the black-backed jackal, now native to eastern and southern Africa, shares ancestry from even farther back with both the African wild dog (*Lycaon pictus*) and the South American bush dog (*Speothos venaticus*). In other words, the latter two dogs are of partly lupine descent. The ancestry of the maned wolf (*Chrysocyon brachyurus*) has still to be unraveled. It is, in fact, more closely related to foxes and to wild dogs than to the genus *Canis*, and it is likely that it evolved in its South American homeland rather than migrating from the north. The same applies to the Andean wolf (*Dusicyon hagenbecki*), which is assigned to the same genus as the fox-like South American zorros (Spanish *zorro*=fox).

PHYSICAL CHARACTERISTICS

The wild canids occur in a wide range of sizes and weights, from the fennec fox (*Fennecus zerda*) of North Africa, which is rarely more than 8in (20cm) high at the shoulder and weighs 3lb (1.4kg) or less, to the largest gray wolf, which may be 36in (91cm) high at the shoulder and weigh, in exceptional cases, 170lb (77kg) or even more. Highly adaptable, different species are able to live in every kind of habitat from the Arctic to the Sahara and Middle Eastern deserts.

SKELETON AND TEETH Canids, like cats, are cursorial (running) rather than ambulatory (walking) animals: that is, their characteristic gait is running as opposed to walking.

Right: The coyote (*Canis latrans*), most adaptable of New World canids, has colonized almost the whole of North America from Alaska to Costa Rica.

Indeed, they are more finely adapted to running — especially running at speed over considerable distances — than any other family among the *Carnivora*; and in this respect, as we shall see in the next chapter, the gray wolf is pre-eminent among canids.

Canids typically have an elongated skull and a long nose. Their powerful cheek muscles enable their jaws to seize, hold and bite their prey efficiently. Most canids have 42 teeth: the upper jaw has (from front to back) six incisors, two canines, eight premolars and four molars; the lower jaw has two additional molars. The large, pointed canines are used to grip and subdue prey. The incisors, at the front of the mouth between and slightly forward of the canines, are used partly to seize and partly to tear flesh. The premolars and molars are involved in reducing food to a state in which it can be swallowed. As already mentioned, the last premolar on each side of the upper jaw and the first molar on each side of the lower jaw are the carnassials, the upper pair being considerably larger than the other premolars. The upper and lower carnassials are so shaped and positioned that they slice through flesh rather like a pair of scissors — an action that requires lateral as well as vertical movement of the jaws in relation to each other. The molars are used not only for chewing flesh but for crushing bones. One expert has calculated that the gray wolf's jaws can exert at least twice as much bone-crushing pressure as that of a German shepherd of the same size.

Two canid exceptions to this pattern of dentition are the raccoon dog (*Nyctereutes procyonoides*) and the dhole (*Cuon alpinus*). The raccoon dog, whose diet includes a

Left: A European gray wolf displays the formidable armory of teeth in its lower jaw. The carnassial is the large tooth between the premolars and molars.

Below: Gray wolves with the carcass of a red deer. Their strong and powerfully muscled jaws enable wolves to crack even the largest bones of their prey.

considerable quantity of insects and fruit as well as small mammals, has an additional molar on each side of the upper jaw, making a total of 44 teeth. The hole has only two true molars on each side of its lower jaw, rather than three as in other canids.

The basic structure of the canid skeleton is similar for almost all the species — a consequence of the fact that most canids are non-specialized in their behavior and lifestyle. A striking feature of their physical make-up is that their limbs are longer in relation to overall body size than those of most other carnivores (a notable exception being the exceptionally fleet-footed cheetah). On the other hand, the relative inflexibility of the canid spine means that, while they are capable of a full progression of movement from a gentle trot to a fast sprint, they do not have the bounding or leaping ability of the cats. Canids, like all carnivores, have seven vertebrae in the neck which are heavily muscled to enable the animal to bring down prey while running. The ribs, which are attached to the thoracic vertebrae (13 or 14, depending on species), are sufficiently long to create the deep chest characteristic of swift-running predators. The skeleton's lumbar region is made up of six to eight vertebrae, while there are three or four vertebrae in the sacrum (the base of the spine). The number of caudal vertebrae making up the tail varies considerably: while the gray wolf has 23, the short-tailed raccoon dog has only 14.

One of the most notable evolutionary changes canid limbs have undergone is the reduction in the number of toes in contact with the ground. In present-day canids the inner-most toe (equivalent to the thumb in man) is located higher up the leg, forming what is known as the dew claw. This sharp claw is useful for striking at and restraining prey. It is absent from the hind limbs of most wild canids but still present in those of most breeds of domestic dogs.

PELAGE Unlike the big cats or, indeed, many domestic breeds of dog, the wild canids show generally monotonal coat colors not only within species but across the family as a whole — the most striking exception to this being the

Right: The colors of a gray wolf's pelage derive from the color of each of its myriad guard hairs, and individual wolves may display a rich variety of shades. Such variation occurs throughout the wolf's range, but most notably among tundra and timber wolves.

African wild dog (*Lycaon pictus*), with its dark, irregular markings against a pale background. On the other hand, the gray wolf, although most commonly a shade of buff, beige, or gray, also occurs in a variety of shades from black to almost pure white. In many species the color of the hairs on the belly and inward-facing parts of the legs may be lighter than that on the rest of the coat, but distinctive markings are confined mainly to the head and tip of the tail which, significantly, play key roles in communication between individuals.

The canid pelage consists of two elements: the long guard hairs forming the visible outer layer that determines its color, and the dense layer of underfur that insulates the animal against the winter cold; the guard hairs tend to throw off rain or other moisture and keep the underfur dry. Cubs born in late winter have a thick coat of underfur, their guard hairs beginning to appear later, in the spring. In most adult wild canids the underfur gradually begins to thin out by molting in spring, and this continues through to the autumn, by which time new underfur has already started to grow.

Page 22: Although white pelts are commonest among wolves of the Arctic, they also occur, along with a variety of color combinations, elsewhere.

Page 23: The remarkable insulating properties of the pelage of the Arctic fox (*Alopex lagopus*) enable it to survive in temperatures as low as -76°F (-60°C).

Below: Pure black coats are quite common in gray wolves, even in latitudes as high as subarctic Alaska and Canada's Northwest Territories.

Right: The size of the pinnae varies from species to species. Those of the Arctic fox are relatively small in order to minimize loss of body heat in the frozen wastes of winter.

THE SENSES

Canids have excellent hearing, eyesight and sense of smell, and they make full use of all three faculties when hunting prey, defending their territories, and communicating with other members of their species.

HEARING The human ear can hear sounds up to a maximum frequency of about 21kHz. At low frequencies canids have similar acoustic perception to man, but they can also perceive sounds that are of a frequency far too high for the human ear to pick up. The coyote, which has perhaps the keenest acoustic perception of all the canids, has an upper frequency limit of 80–85kHz, while domestic hunting dogs have a limit of about 60kHz.

The pinnae or ear flaps — that is, the visible parts of a canid's ears — can be moved so as to enable the animal to locate the exact direction from which a sound is coming and also, in varying degrees depending on the canid species, the distance of the sound source. Coyotes frequently catch small rodents that may be motionless and invisible under several inches of undisturbed snow. It is almost certain that they can hear such quarry, although their sense of smell may also play a part here.

The size of the pinnae varies from species to species. Those of the Arctic fox are relatively small in order to minimize loss of body heat in the frozen wastes of winter. By contrast the fennec fox has enormous pinnae, which not only help to radiate excess body heat in its scorching desert habitat but also help to fix with remarkable precision the location of small prey such as insects and grubs that may lie concealed in the sand.

SIGHT Many canids hunt by night as well as by day and so need — like cats and other carnivores — to have acute vision

Left: The gray wolf's relatively small pinnae (ear-flaps) are typical of canids native to the cool high latitudes.

Above: By contrast, the enormous ear-flaps of the bat-eared fox (*Otocyon megalotis*) of tropical East Africa help it to dissipate heat from its body; they also aid in pinpointing the location of its mainly insect prey.

in a wide range of light conditions. The retina of the canid eye consists of two types of cells, called rods and cones. The rods give acuity in poor light conditions but lose their sensitivity in bright daylight and are unable to distinguish colors. The cones are sensitive to bright light and, in some measure, to colors, but they lose most of their sensitivity in weak light. The color-sensitivity of canid eyes is inferior to those of humans, and it is likely that in daylight canid vision is less acute than man's. On the other hand, it is believed that wolves and some other canids are able to see and follow rapid movements rather better than man. Like cats, but unlike humans, canids have an important secondary aid to night vision. Immediately behind the canid retina is a structure called the *tapetum lucidum*. Any light passing through the retina that has not been intercepted by the cells is reflected back from the tapetum onto the rods, which thus have a second opportunity to respond to it.

The canid's hunting skills are aided significantly by its having binocular vision. Coupled with its visual acuity in following swiftly moving visual signals, this enables the predator to interpret the overlapping images received by each eye and thus to determine exactly when to strike at a rapidly retreating prey. Moreover, its eyes are set wide on the head, giving it a much wider field of view than man's.

SMELL Canids have a stronger and more finely discriminating sense of smell than man's: they live in an olfactory environment of whose richness and subtlety we can only guess. Every object, however small, whether animate or inanimate, whether friend, foe or prey, is perceived more comprehensively by their olfactory apparatus than by any of their other senses. Blind canids, including wolves, are able to find their way about in unfamiliar surroundings and, if downwind, wolves are capable of picking up the scent of their ungulate prey over distances of a mile or more. Dogs bred specifically for their acute sense of smell, such as bloodhounds, can follow scent trails that are several days old.

The canid's ability to distinguish between a vast range of scent signals depends on the nature of the olfactory apparatus within its elongated snout, an apparatus that is relatively larger in canids than in cats and some other carnivores. The olfactory organ is made up of turbinals — a group of bones whose surface area is enormous in relation to its overall size because it is made up of a complex arrangement of coils and spirals. The surface of the turbinals is coated in olfactory mucous membrane. The whole area has a battery of nerves that enable olfactory information to be passed to the brain.

A more specialized olfactory structure, known as Jacobsen's organ, deals mainly with scent signals from canids of the same species as the recipient. This is a pouch-like structure lined with receptor cells similar to those in the turbinals and is situated in the roof the mouth behind the upper incisor teeth. It is believed to be involved, among other things, in detecting olfactory signals from females in oestrus. An acute sense of smell is obviously important to an animal that has to hunt down its prey. But it is also important in enabling canids to perceive and recognize the scent of, for instance, the glandular secretions and urine sprays with which canids mark out their territories or advertise their presence.

WILD CANIDS AND MAN

For many hundreds of years Western man — that is to say, societies based on European cultural traditions — has regarded the wolf not only as a pest but as a creature of nightmares, of "darkness and blood." For many millennia from the end of the last ice age, some 10,000 years ago, gray wolves and men were in direct competition for survival in the Holarctic. Today, such competition persists in far northern latitudes inhabited by native American hunting peoples and

Right: The eyes of canids, such as this red fox's, are set well apart at the front of the head, giving them a wide field of view as well as binocular vision.

Below: While the gray wolf's color vision is inferior to man's, its eyes are better at picking up and following rapid movements.

WOLVES

their Eurasian cousins. But on the whole such people bear the wolf none of the hatred heaped upon it by their supposedly more civilized neighbors to the south. Rather, many of them regard the wolf as a competitor that they may need to kill but also as a predator from which they may learn refinements to their own hunting skills.

Until the development of guns, man and wolf competed on more or less equal terms. But over the past few hundred years not only guns but an increasingly sophisticated range of technology has been brought to bear on what has become a struggle weighted heavily in favor of man. White settlers changed the pattern of the man-wolf rivalry in North America by killing or driving out the ungulates on which the wolves

Left: Wolves, like some hunting dogs, have a sense of smell whose acuity and range is far superior to man's. Much of their interpretation of the world about them is based on olfactory signals. This gray wolf pauses to pick up a scent on the trail.

Below: A Mexican wolf sniffs the scent of urine sprayed by itself (or by another wolf) on a tree to mark out the boundary of, or a route within, its territory.

preyed and using the land for raising cattle or sheep. The wolf, deprived of its natural prey, began to kill the settlers' livestock. And so the long campaign to exterminate the gray wolf from North America began.

The first bounty on wolf skins was declared by the Pilgrim Fathers in New England in the 1630s. The campaign to eradicate what stock farmers regard as simply a vicious pest has continued unabated ever since. In 1909 the U.S. Congress responded to mounting pressure from cattle and sheep farmers by launching a pest and predator program to wipe out all wild carnivores that might be suspected of offering any kind of threat to farm livestock. The eradication program continues today, carried out by hunters and trappers of the animal-control branch of the U.S. Department of Agriculture. The branch has an enormous variety of methods and weapons at its disposal — guns, traps, poisons; hunting dogs, snowmobiles, and light planes and helicopters. State agencies, individual farmers, and self-styled sportsmen pitch in to help.

It is a scandalous and disgusting campaign. It has also

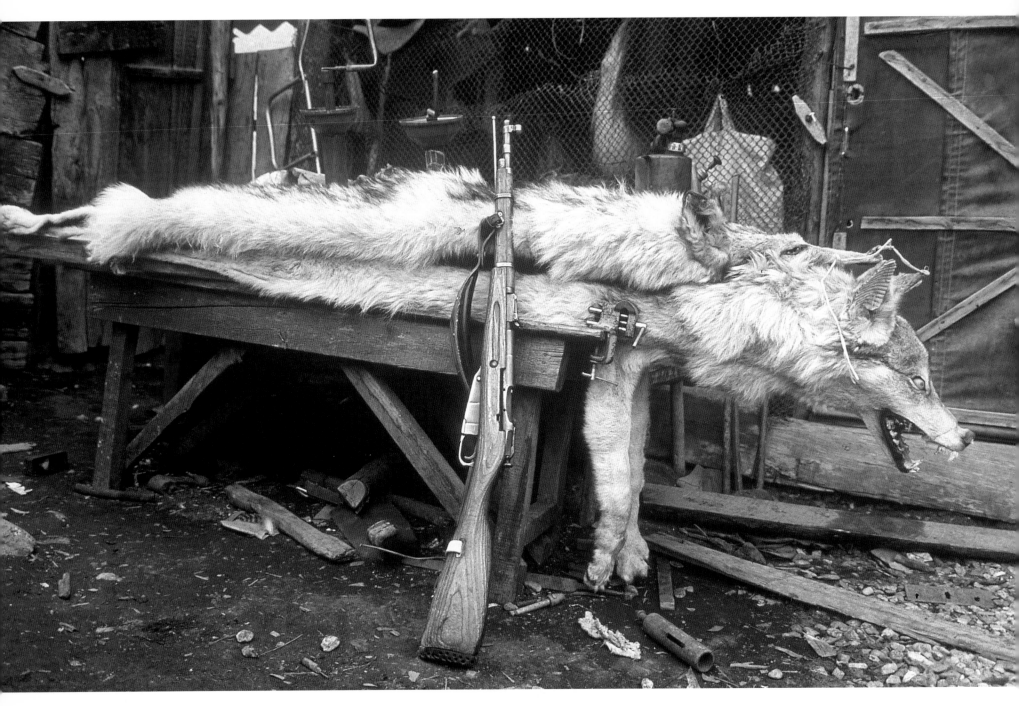

Above: The carcass of a gray wolf shot by herdsmen in Mongolia, where wolves once preyed on bactrian camels used as beasts of burden and have been hunted almost to extinction.

Right: A captive wolf-dog hybrid bitch. Almost all the very few authenticated attacks by wolves on people have been by hybrids, probably infected by rabies. In the wild, healthy wolves instinctively shun any contact with man.

been, in important respects, a total failure. The main target in recent years has been the coyote. But while the gray wolf has been eliminated from almost everywhere in the United States, the coyote (in spite of the fact that 60,000 and more are killed each year) has substantially increased both in num- bers and in range, and it has moved into habitats formerly occupied by its larger gray cousin. (In the former Soviet Union a similarly disgraceful, and equally unsuccessful, extermination campaign was waged against the gray wolf before and after World War 2.) Like the red fox, the coyote prospers in North America in spite of man's best efforts to consign it to oblivion. Meanwhile the gray wolf, although its range has shrunk dramatically over the past 150 years, con- tinues to survive in wild, thinly inhabited regions of the Holarctic in North America and Eurasia, and also in many steppe and semi-desert regions of the Old World.

WOLVES

The Gray Wolf

THE GRAY WOLF

The gray wolf is the largest of all the canids, although its size varies appreciably in different parts of its range. As we have mentioned, the largest are found in Alaska and northern Canada, where individual males may weigh 170lb (77kg) and more — twice the weight of a typical German shepherd — although even in these areas the average weight of males is 90–110lb (41–50kg); females typically weigh 15–20lb (7–9kg) less. The smallest gray is the Arabian, which may weigh 45lb (20kg) or less.

RANGE: THEN AND NOW

That the gray wolf is highly adaptable as to both habitat and prey animals is attested by the remarkable range of environments in which it is capable of flourishing, from sub-arctic wastes to semi-desert. Its original range in the New World once included the whole of North America, from the northernmost tip of Greenland southwards almost as far as Mexico City. Today there are small, isolated communities in Mexico, but it is likely that they are too few and too small to remain

Above: The gray wolf is narrower in the chest and longer in the legs than the superficially similar German shepherd.

Right: A Canadian wolf pack on the trail in search of prey. A pack's territory may extend over several hundred square miles and it will be fiercely defended against encroachment by other packs.

Pages 34–35: A timber wolf in hot pursuit of prey is capable of prodigious leaps over obstacles such as this stream.

WOLVES

viable for much longer. The gray wolf has been wiped out from the whole of the United States, with the exception of Alaska, which has a population of about 20,000, and small but thriving communities in Minnesota's Superior National Park, Isle Royale National Park in Michigan, northwestern Montana and elsewhere in the neighborhood of the Canadian border.

Canada has probably between 25,000 and 30,000 gray wolves distributed throughout the country except for New Brunswick and Newfoundland. The largest numbers, though not the densest populations, are in the Northwest Territories. The remainder are mainly in the northern halves of the provinces of British Columbia, Alberta, Saskatchewan, Manitoba and northern and eastern Quebec, including Labrador.

The gray wolf was once abundant throughout Europe. While it had been exterminated in England by the 1480s, Shakespeare could still refer to "the howling of Irish wolves against the moon" in *As You Like It*, which was written about 1598; indeed the last wolves disappeared from both Ireland and Scotland only in the mid- to late 18th century. The wolf has also disappeared from many other western European countries. In Spain and Portugal, where it roamed throughout the peninsula until the mid-19th century, it is now confined to isolated parts of northwestern Spain and to the central areas of the borderlands between the two countries. In Italy a once-thriving population has been drastically reduced, since World War 2, to about 200, mainly in the Abruzzo section of the central Appennino range, where they are now protected.

In Poland, where it is given limited protection as a game animal, the wolf population of about 1,000 is mainly in the east near the Russian border, and in the southeast in the Beskrdy mountains (part of the Carpathian range), whence they migrate into neighboring Slovakia. To the north, wolves are almost extinct in Norway and Sweden and there are perhaps 80 or 90 left in Finland.

To the south, in the Balkans, the situation varies greatly

Above Left: A captive European common wolf (*Canis lupus lupus*), a medium-sized subspecies of the North American gray wolf.

Left: A white Canadian wolf. Despite its color, this individual's territory was well to the south of the tundra.

Right: A large gray wolf at rest in its home territory in the mountain forests of Montana.

from country to country. In Romania there is a thriving population of about 2,000, mainly in the Carpathians, where they prey on roe deer and wild boar. In Bulgaria, however, there are fewer than 100, and they have been replaced in many areas by the golden jackal (*Canis aureus*), which preys largely on farm stock. The conflict in the former Yugoslavia has had a catastrophic effect on local wolf populations. In Croatia the Serbian army extended its policy of "ethnic cleansing" to embrace animals of every kind, including wolves and their ungulate prey, though small populations of both survived in some reserves and national parks. In Greece the population is 400-500; many wolves are still shot or poisoned every year, but there are viable populations in a number of protected areas in the central and northern mountains. Finally, in Turkey wolves are found in small numbers in southern and eastern regions of the country, where local populations are supplemented by migrants from Armenia, Azerbaijan, and Iran. The wolves are not generally protected but hunting them has been outlawed in national parks and nature reserves.

In the Middle Eastern countries of Lebanon, Syria, Jordan and Iraq small numbers of desert-dwelling wolves eke out an existence in areas where their natural prey have been ousted by sheep and goats. Their future is bleak here: they have been ruthlessly hunted because they have been forced to prey on the domestic stock, which are overgrazing the land and encouraging the process of erosion and desertification. There is a similar problem in parts of Iran, but elsewhere in the country wolves inhabit areas of steppe and deciduous forest, and they are also protected in several national parks and reserves. Israel is the only country in the Middle East to confer general protection on wolves. In the north of the country, in the area of the Golan Heights, there are small populations of relatively large wolves, while distinctly smaller ones are found in some central areas. The small Arabian wolf is found in areas on the margins of true desert in Arabia, the Sinai peninsula and southern Jordan.

There are perhaps 2,000 wolves on the Indian subconti-

Right: A Canadian wolf in its full winter coat. Wolves from the most northerly parts of the species' range have a much longer and denser fur than those living farther south.

Pages 42–43: The light and dark elements of this captive Mexican gray wolf's coat help it to blend into the dappled light of its woodland home.

WOLVES

A European common wolf in the Mazury lakeland region in the northeastern corner of Poland, where wolves are given partial protection as game animals.

Above: With the partly eaten carcass of a red deer it has killed.

Right: It snarls at an intruder, its face expressing a mixture of aggression and some anxiety.

Below: It starts to drag the carcass away to a place of concealment.

nent and the population is endangered by local eradication campaigns and by the reduction of the wolf's natural habitat by the spread of agriculture and by land-development schemes. Although wolves are relatively safe in a number of national parks and nature reserves, the margins of many of these areas are being encroached upon by farmers in search of grazing.

Wolves once roamed all over China, but in the 20th century the pressures of a rising human population and the expansion of agriculture has led to their elimination from the central, eastern and southern regions of the country. In the far west, in Xinjiang (Sinkiang) province, the huge Taxkorgan nature reserve, close to where China's frontiers with Pakistan, Afghanistan, and Tadzhikistan meet in the towering ramparts of the Pamir, the wolf's ancient habitat in the deep valleys has been devastated by overgrazing by domesticated animals, which ousted the much more stable populations of ungulates on which the wolves preyed. In

WOLVES

many areas of China fear of rabies led to a bounty on wolves being declared, and thousands of wolves have been killed by shooting or poisoning. More hopeful, however, is the development of the enormous reserve in Qing-zang (Chang-tang), in northwestern Tibet, where great efforts are being made to maintain the natural flora and fauna of the mountains and valleys. In Mongolia, China's northern neighbor, wolves have been hunted almost to extinction in the Great Gobi national park after wolves had severely depleted the population of wild bactrian camels over a period of some years (the camels are caught and tamed by the Mongolians for use as beasts of burden).

The world's largest population of wolves is to be found in European and Asiatic Russia. In spite of vigorous campaigns to control or eradicate it in stock-farming regions — probably two million have been killed since the late 1920s — the wolf is still as numerous as ever. An accurate assessment of numbers is impossible; it is likely that the total population exceeds 200,000, and it may be rising in some regions. In the taiga, for instance, the international demand for timber has led to massive clearance of huge areas of the great northern forests, which revert to scrub and rough grassland. These areas are being colonised by ungulates such as elk and deer, and as their numbers increase, so do those of the wolves that prey on them.

WOLF SUBSPECIES AND RACES

It is now generally accepted by taxonomists that all the gray wolves of both the Old World and the New belong to the same species, *Canis lupus*. Some 32 or 33 subspecies — 24 in North America and eight or nine in Eurasia — have been proposed, but it is unlikely that all of them have strict taxonomic validity. For one thing, several of the subspecies have been proposed mainly on the basis either of their geographical range or the coat colors of living or dead specimens. Neither of these criteria is as reliable a basis for classification as differences in, say, the size and shape of the skull and brain case or in other morphological features. There is no question but that individuals from one supposed subspecies

Right: A pair of European wolves in their summer coats in the Highland Wildlife Park, near Kincraig, Scotland – the sort of terrain in which wolves ranged free until the last of their wild ancestors were eradicated from Scotland in the 18th century.

WOLVES

interbreed with individuals from another in areas where their two ranges overlap; and this "mongrelization" has no doubt been going on for millennia. Again, it might seem sensible to use coat color as a basis for classification, until one has actually seen a wolf pack: in many cases the individuals in a pack will have a variety of coat colors, from creamy white, say, through gray to black. The latest taxonomic thinking suggests that there may be only five authentic subspecies in North America. What can be said with certainty is that seven of the originally proposed North American subspecies (mainly from the United States) and two of the Eurasian (from Japan) are now extinct.

Nonetheless, there are two groups of North American gray wolves, embracing many of the accepted subspecies, that can usually be distinguished on the basis of general appearance: the tundra wolves and the timber wolves. On average, the tundra wolves have longer and more luxuriant coats, which are noticeably lighter in color (although black tundra wolves are not uncommon), whereas the timber wolves, whose ranges are farther south on the margins of the great boreal forests, are commonly darkish gray to black (although they, too vary in color); the timber wolves also have more pointed ears than those of the tundra races. Some subspecies (as noted below) are found in both tundra and taiga, but even among these the more northerly members of the race will on average have lighter-colored coats than those farther south.

NORTH AMERICAN SUBSPECIES The New World gray wolves are most abundant in Alaska and the Northwest Territories of Canada. In most parts of their range in North America they are thinly spread out and confined to areas well away from the main centres of human settlement. It is generally accepted that wolves avoid areas where the density of the human population is more than three per square mile (2.6sq km)

The most northerly of the 17 existing subspecies is the whitish gray Greenland wolf (*Canis lupus orion*), which is

Right: A captive Mexican subspecies of the gray wolf. Although it once roamed over much of northern Mexico, it is now on the verge of extinction in the wild.

Pages 50 and 51: White coats are found among both tundra and timber wolves. The ears of this individual, somewhat smaller and rounder than those typical of the southern races, show this to be a tundra wolf.

49

also found on smaller islands adjacent to Baffin. It is the smallest of the Arctic wolves. To the west is the Banks Island tundra wolf (*C. l. bernardi*), a large white wolf with black-tipped hairs along the top of its back. West again, in the Arctic coast region of Alaska, is the Alaska tundra wolf (*C. l. tundarum*), a very large wolf with a long, light-gray coat. Its even larger, but closely related, neighbour to the south is the interior Alaska wolf (*C. l. pambasileus*), which occurs throughout Alaska except for the Arctic coast, and also in Yukon Territory to the east. Another very large subspecies, the Kennai Peninsula wolf (*C. l. alces*), is named after its restricted habitat on the Gulf of Alaska to the south of Anchorage. It is interesting to speculate whether its exceptional size has anything to do with the fact that in this area its main prey, the moose (*Alces alces*), is also noticeably larger than in many other regions.

The medium-sized, usually white or buff-coloured Mackenzie tundra wolf (*C. l. mackenzii*) is found along the Arctic coast of Canada's Northwest Territories to the east of the Mackenzie River and as far south as Great Bear Lake. To the east again, the Hudson Bay wolf (*C. l. hudsonicus*), of similar size and pelage and perhaps taxonomically indistinguishable from the Mackenzie race, is found along the Arctic coast north-west of Hudson Bay, but it also ranges into the great evergreen forests of northern Manitoba to the west of the bay. The last of the existing tundra subspecies of North America is the Labrador wolf (*C. l. labradorius*), which is found throughout Labrador and northern Quebec province. As with the Hudson Bay wolf, its range includes the tundra in the north and the boreal forests farther south.

The North American subspecies with, historically, the greatest range is the eastern timber wolf (*C. l. lycaon*), which formerly occurred over much of eastern Canada and the United States from the southern shore of Hudson Bay in the north to Florida in the south. Today its range is restricted to southern Quebec, Ontario, the eastern margins of

found on the northern coast of Greenland. Very similar in size and color and found on the large group, known as the Elizabeth Islands, immediately to the west of northern Greenland, is the Melville Island wolf (*C. l. arctos*). These two wolves are probably indistinguishable subspecifically. To the south is the Baffin Island wolf (*C. l. manningi*), which is

Above Left: Autumn tints the foliage — and after the long summer molt this young captive adult has acquired its new coat, which will continue to grow until the onset of winter.

Right: Although black individuals occur in varicolored packs, distinct black phases are commonest among the subspecies native to western Canada and the Alaskan interior.

Manitoba, and parts of the northern extremities of Minnesota and Michigan. One of the smallest North American wolves, its coat is typically a mixture of dark and lighter grays, though both white and black individuals are not uncommon.

Smallest of Alaska's wolves is the Alexander Archipelago timber wolf (*C. l. ligoni*), which occurs on several of the 1,000-odd islands that form part of the southerly extension of the state, and also on the neighboring mainland north of the city of Juneau. It has a darker pelage with shorter guard hairs than other races in this part of North America and also a higher proportion of completely black-coated individuals than most other subspecies. Immediately to the east, occurring almost throughout British Columbia, is the timber wolf (*C. l. columbianus*) named after the province. A large wolf, it is usually dark gray in color but, again, black individuals often feature in a pack. Somewhat lighter gray in color and smaller in size, the Vancouver Island wolf (*C. l. crassodon*) is confined to that island.

Probably the largest of all the Canadian wolves is the Mackenzie valley wolf (*C. l. occidentalis*), whose range extends from eastern sub-arctic Yukon Territory south through eastern British Columbia and western and central Alberta as far south as Edmonton. The color of these wolves varies considerably not only (as might be expected) over its considerable north-to-south range but also within local populations. Finally, in the eastern margins of Alberta, much of Saskatchewan north of Saskatoon, and western Manitoba almost as far south as Winnipeg, an elusive medium- to large-sized subspecies, named *C. l. griseoalbus* in the mid-19th century but still of problematic taxonomic status, is reported to vary in colour (as its subspecific name suggests) from white to darkish grey.

The only other surviving North American subspecies of gray wolf, and the smallest of all, is the Mexican (*C. l. baileyi*). Typically of a dark greyish colour, the lobo (as it is known locally) occurs in small numbers in isolated communities in Mexico's Sierra Madre range and neighboring areas

in the west of the country. Rarely seen nowadays in numbers of more than one or two at a time, it is in extreme danger of extinction.

EURASIAN SUBSPECIES The different ranges of most gray wolf subspecies in the Old World correspond approximately to the broad bands of natural vegetation, determined by climate and topography, that run for thousands of miles from eastern Europe to the shores of the Pacific. The northernmost subspecies, the tundra wolf (*Canis lupus albus*), ranges from the northern tip of Scandinavia in the west to Bering Strait in the east. Although it occurs mainly above the Arctic Circle (67.5°N) — notably in Russia's Taymyr Peninsula, where it preys on the large herds of reindeer (*Rangifer tarandus*, the same species as the North American caribou) — it is also found in the forested regions farther south in eastern Siberia and the Kamchatka Peninsula. It is similar in appearance and size to the large Alaska tundra wolf.

The common wolf (*C. l. lupus*) is the subspecies of timber wolf that once ranged throughout Europe and on margins of the the immense belt of taiga (evergreen forest) that in Russia and Siberia extends from the Arctic Circle southwards to approximately 55°N in its western half and 50°N in the east. Medium-sized, with dark fur, the common wolf preys on reindeer and elk (the same species as the North American moose, *Alces alces*, but somewhat smaller), and also on beaver and Arctic hare.

The arid grasslands of the Eurasian steppe extend from the plains of eastern Romania through Ukraine and Russia south of the Urals and on towards the Mongolian and Chinese frontiers. The steppe wolf (*C. l. campestris*) is a small animal with coarse, brownish gray pelage. Over much of the eastern part of its range the ungulate population has been almost wiped out by human predation. For instance, this subspecies once preyed extensively on the saiga antelope in western Kazakhstan, but the saiga is now almost extinct in the wild, and the wolves now prey mainly on rodents such as bobak (steppe marmot), suslik (*Citellus*, a ground squirrel), gerbils and voles.

South of the Eurasian steppe an even larger but intermittent belt of scrub, semi-desert, desert, and arid high plateaus and mountain valleys stretches from Turkey eastwards

Right: The wolf uses its ears, forehead, eyes, lips and teeth in certain ways to communicate a considerable range of feelings, especially those to do with hierarchy within the pack.

Pages 56–57: When not engaged in displays of dominance or submission, wolves are usually friendly and companionable with other members of the pack.

WOLVES

through the Middle East, central Asia and onwards to the eastern margins of Mongolia. This is the realm of the Tibetan wolf (*C. l. chanco*), a medium-sized subspecies with long, light gray or brownish-gray pelage. Sharing the easternmost part of this range, and also found in the northern half of China, is the Chinese wolf (*C. l. laniger*), of similar size and color but with somewhat more woolly coat (its subspecific name comes from the Latin *laniger*=wool-bearing). Some authorities believe these two wolves are local variants of a single subspecies.

South of the ranges of the Tibetan and Chinese wolves is that of the South Asian wolf (*C. l. pallipes*), which occurs in steppe and semi-desert areas extending from the eastern shores of the Mediterranean through central Israel, Jordan, Iraq, Iran, Afghanistan and Pakistan, and on into areas of dry tropical forest in northern India. Somewhat smaller than the Chinese wolf, it has short, medium- to light brown pelage. In many parts of its range the ungulates that are its natural prey have been ousted by domestic sheep and goats that now are perforce its chief source of food. It is vigorously hunted throughout its range except in Iran's game reserves and national parks, which offer a good chance of its survival in the wild.

Finally, the smallest of all the subspecies, the pale desert wolf (*C. l. arabs*), is found in southern Jordan, the southern half of the Sinai peninsula and in parts of the Arabian peninsula. A solitary hunter, it lives mainly on the margins of true desert, preying on rodents, foxes and any carrion it can find. Weighing no more than 45lb (20kg) at most and with short, wiry, sandy-colored coat, it bears scant resemblance to the gray wolves of the great northern forests and tundra. Unlike most, if not all, of the other subspecies, it has never been known to howl; and this may be connected with the fact that the desert wolf does not live in a pack.

Pages 58–59: Wolves howl, like this pair, for a variety of reasons: to warn members of other packs encroaching on their territory, to summon members of their own pack — or often, seemingly, for the pure pleasure of having a communal singsong.

Right: When on the trail in deep snow, wolves move in single file, usually but not always led by the alpha male or female. Unlike the gait of almost all large dogs, a wolf's front and hind legs on each side swing in the same line, allowing the hind foot to land in the track made by the front foot — an important aid to ease of movement in snow.

THE WOLF PACK

We shall be dealing here mainly with the northern subspecies — the gray wolves of the taiga and tundra — which have been studied much more intensively than the others. A carnivore that preys on large mammals must either be as large as its prey (or nearly so) or it must hunt in groups. The gray wolf, like the African wild dog (*Lycaon pictus*), is a group hunter. (It is true that a single large timber wolf may on occasion kill a moose or caribou, but hunting in packs is a much more efficient, and less hazardous, method of dealing with large ungulate prey.)

THE MAKE-UP OF THE PACK Because they determine the method by which gray wolves hunt and are able to survive their often hazardous existence, the pack and its organization are central to the life of the species. A pack is almost invariably made up of a male and female and their offspring, although it may from time to time temporarily include a close relative of the mated pair. A pack usually has its beginnings in the meeting and courtship of two young adult wolves who have left the pack, or packs, in which they were raised in order to find a new territory. Alternatively, two individuals (perhaps from the same pack) may first pair up and then seek their own territory. Either way, once it has been established, the territory will be defended fiercely against intruders, whether individual wolves or packs.

Each year, a new litter adds to the size of the pack. Gray wolves reach sexual maturity at 22 months; and while some of the young may leave the pack (or be killed or die of disease) before the end of their second year, others may stay for as long as four years, by which time the pack may number up to 20 or more individuals of various ages. Large packs, then, may include several adults of each sex. But the original breeding pair — the *alpha* male and female, as they are called — remain dominant within each pack.

Right: When on the trail in search of prey, members of a pack will often fan out in woodland to improve the chances of a sighting.

Pages 62–63: Four members of a pack of European common wolves: the alpha male and female (centre and rear, left) and two younger, subordinate males.

Page 66: A young white timber wolf on the lookout for winter prey.

Page 67: A white timber wolf in magnificent full winter coat.

DOMINANCE AND SUBORDINATION Interestingly, the social structure within the pack is different from that in, say, a pride of lions. In the case of the latter, dominance is exerted exclusively by the leading male. In the wolf pack, however, the social structure is based on a hierarchy within each gender: the alpha male dominates the other males, and the alpha female dominates the other females. During the mating season, the alpha male will fight to prevent other males from mating with the alpha female, and the alpha female will fight to keep other females in oestrus from mating with the alpha male. The alpha male, however, will not necessarily have dominance over the alpha female, and several observers have remarked on the fact that in some packs the alpha female is clearly the leader.

The concepts of dominance and hierarchy become rather elusive if one attempts to apply them mechanically to life in the wolf pack. They are certainly evident during the mating season in the way described above, but even then they are not always apparent: on occasions an alpha female will mate

Above: Although both wolves appear to be snarling aggressively, the flattened ears of the one at right shows it to be submissive.

Right: The two wolves in the center submit to the authority of the alpha male (right) and alpha female.

Pages 68–69: Two young males of subordinate status test their relative positions in the pack hierarchy.

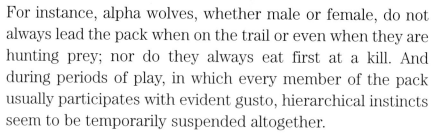

For instance, alpha wolves, whether male or female, do not always lead the pack when on the trail or even when they are hunting prey; nor do they always eat first at a kill. And during periods of play, in which every member of the pack usually participates with evident gusto, hierarchical instincts seem to be temporarily suspended altogether.

Nevertheless, it is clear that such flexibility and informality in behavior is made possible only because it is underlain by a social structure that serves to bind the pack. At the top of the structure are the alpha male and alpha female, who may be four to six years old (although wolves in zoos occasionally live to a maximum of 16 years, in the wild few survive longer than half that span). Below them are subordinate males and females of various ages, some of whom are sexually mature. Subordinates establish an order of dominance within each sex; the beta male and beta female will usually be two or three years old, depending on the age of the pack as a whole, and the least dominant will be the yearlings. The wolf pups constitute the third element in the pack hierarchy. They also establish an order of dominance, but this one temporarily embraces both males and females.

Packs vary considerably in size. One of the largest reported in North America, in 1967, contained 36 members, and packs of 12 or more are not uncommon in certain regions; but the average number is much lower — varying from eight to the bare minimum of two. Pack size depends on various factors. These include the relative abundance of prey animals in a pack's territory; the smallest number of wolves needed to find and kill the prey (this obviously depends partly on the size of their usual prey animal); the largest number of wolves whose hunger could be satisfied by a single kill; and the maximum number of members with whom each wolf can form social bonds.

Above: "Riding up" involves a dominant wolf placing his forelegs across the shoulders of a subordinate. If the latter fails to submit, the dominant wolf may gently but firmly bite its neck.

Page 72: Lowered tails as well as flattened ears show two wolves submitting in response to the dominating, though hardly aggressive, stare of the wolf at left.

Page 73: Subordinate members of a pack greet a dominant wolf who has returned from a hunt.

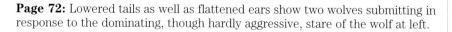

with a beta (second-ranking) male without overt objections from the alpha male. They are also evident when the pack is making a killing, when its territory is being defended against intruders, and on other occasions when the cohesion of the pack needs to be reinforced. At other times, however, there is much more flexibility in the collective behavior of the pack.

COMMUNICATION The social structure of the pack, then, is quite complex, and it is defined and maintained by a variety of means of communication: vocal, what might be called body language, and scent-marking.

The wolf's best-known means of vocal expression is howling, which is normally indulged in by every member of the pack, including young pups, and has a number of quite distinct purposes. First, a pack will howl collectively in response to the howling of another pack. This, usually, is an expression

Above: Dominance behavior may vary greatly in intensity, depending on the situation. Without resorting to the overtly aggressive gesture of bearing the teeth in its upper jaw, the wolf at left nonetheless elicits submissive behavior from the one on the right.

of territoriality: "No trespassing!" It is most commonly heard when the pack has just made a kill or if the alien pack is approaching too close to a den with young pups. Another function of howling is for wolves to communicate with other members of their own pack. It is used when, for instance, pack members have become separated in the course of pursuing prey, perhaps over difficult terrain or through forests, and those who have made the kill want the rest of the pack to join them.

A third function is bound up with maintaining the cohesion of the pack and with its hierarchical structure. This kind of howling session is usually followed by displays of dominance behavior by alpha and beta members of the pack, accompanied by other vocal expressions, such as growling

and whining, by various pack members, depending on their social status. Once the dominance hierarchy has been asserted in this way, however, the pack will often indulge in an energetic session of play. Howling of this kind is heard most frequently during the winter season of courtship and breeding.

It seems clear from the reports of many observers that wolves take a particular delight in howling and that, once it starts, it spreads like wildfire through the pack. One observer has described such "chorus howling" as being the lupine equivalent of community singing. Even humans who can do a rough and ready imitation of a wolf howl can elicit a response from a pack, and some national parks in Canada where there are wolves operate wolf-howling tours in the summer. The naturalist Adolph Murie, one of the foremost authorities on the North American gray wolf, wrote vividly of an occasion when he watched four adult wolves playing together, tails wagging. After a while they started to howl, and almost

WOLVES

immediately they were joined by a female who had been resting with her pups in a den nearby. Her arrival triggered another bout of tail-wagging, after which all five began to howl. After a few minutes, the howling ceased as abruptly as it had begun, the female trotted back to her pups, and the others departed, presumably on a hunt for food.

A howl can take various forms, but it usually begins with a glissando, starting low and rising sharply, and then slowly falling. When other wolves join in they may either harmonize on the first wolf's note or produce striking discords. Either way, the sound is hauntingly beautiful — but of a kind of beauty that sends a shiver up the spine on a dark winter's night. In the still, cold air of the Arctic, the sound can carry for six miles and more.

Like dogs, wolves can growl, bark, whimper and make other sounds as well as howl, but these are usually connected with displays of dominance or submission. Body language — that is, postural communication — plays a central role in these displays. Indeed, an individual wolf's relationship with every other member of the pack is manifested by this form of

Above: A typically submissive posture: lowered head, partly closed eyes, flattened ears and lowered tail.

Right: Reinforcing submissive behavior: a dominant adult (center) gently takes the neck of a wolf cub between its jaws.

Page 76–77: This type of submissive behavior is a throwback to, and an imitation of, the way young cubs attempt to lick the muzzle of an adult wolf to make it regurgitate food.

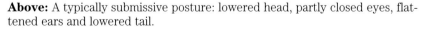

WOLVES

communication, and by it the wolf is able to express a wide range and intensity of emotions. Body language is found in all the canids, but it has developed most fully in both range and subtlety among the group-living species.

Postural signals involve the whole of the wolf's body in some degree, but the most important areas are the head — specifically the mouth and teeth, the forehead, and the ears — and the tail. An alpha wolf may not need to do anything more than stare fixedly at a subordinate to make the latter evince submissive behavior. Intensified dominance behavior may involve snarling, an open jaw with bared teeth, the corners of the mouth pulled forward, erect ears pointed forward, wrinkling of the forehead, hackles raised, and half-raised tail. The subordinate will usually respond with a closed, "grinning" mouth with lips drawn back, eyes almost closed, ears drawn back and flattened, and tail held between the back legs. In an even more emphatically submissive response, the subordinate may flatten itself on the ground, or roll over onto its side or back. Alternatively the alpha

Right: Even full-grown wolves will indulge in the face-licking gesture to acknowledge their subordinate status.

Below: A dominant male seizes the muzzle of a subordinate adult. Its expression may look fierce, but the action is not designed to draw blood.

WOLVES

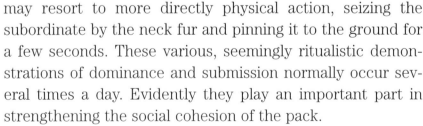

may resort to more directly physical action, seizing the subordinate by the neck fur and pinning it to the ground for a few seconds. These various, seemingly ritualistic demonstrations of dominance and submission normally occur several times a day. Evidently they play an important part in strengthening the social cohesion of the pack.

Such overt rehearsals of dominance behavior are, in a sense, the extremes of postural expression among gray wolves; there are many other forms that bear witness to the variety and subtlety of the means of visual communication within the pack. For instance, a subordinate will often beg for food from an alpha by lifting its muzzle, with mouth closed but with the lips drawn back, and tentatively paw at the alpha's muzzle.

Above: Communal howling, as here, is usually started by one wolf, the others quickly joining in at the beginning of the leader's second howl. A pack rarely howls in unison, preferring harmonies or discords, and the haunting sound can be heard for several miles.

Right: When howling, a wolf draws its lips forward and points its muzzle skywards. A howling session, whether by an individual or by several wolves, may last from about 30 seconds to a few minutes.

Pages 82–83: An extreme expression of dominance behavior: an alpha male pins a subordinate wolf to the ground, its jaws around the subordinate's throat. If, as here, the subordinate wolf submits, it will soon be released unhurt.

The third method of communication, scent-marking, is concerned, like some aspects of howling, with territoriality: the boundaries of a pack's territory are delineated by scent-markings that are regularly renewed and act as a warning to neighboring packs not to trespass. The scent may include not

only urine or faeces but secretions from the anal gland, the supracaudal gland at the base of the tail, and glands on the cheeks and between the toes. Wolves establish a network of routes within their territories, and the territorial boundaries, as well as important route junctions within the territory, are re-marked with scent at least once every two or three weeks.

Scent-marking has traditionally been regarded as essentially a warning to other wolf packs. More recently it has been suggested that it is, just as importantly, a guide for the resident pack, especially for its younger members. Wolves inspect scent-marks every two or three minutes when on the move, using their extraordinary powers of olfactory discrimination to interpret the "message" in each mark. Such inspections tell a wolf whether other members of the pack, perhaps on a hunt, have passed this way; and they can tell very accurately, from the strength of the scent signal, exactly when the other wolves were there. A series of such scent-marks of the same age will, for instance, serve to guide a wolf to the spot where other members of the pack have cached a recent kill. Moreover, a scent-mark is rather like an ID card: other members of the pack can identify the marker by the particular odour of an individual mark. Remarkably, scent-marks — often in the form of faeces — are also used to identify dangerous objects to other members of a pack: they have been found on wolf traps and even on poisoned baits.

Above: A European male wolf preparing to mate with a female in oestrus. Mating usually takes place in late winter or early spring.

Right: A female warms her pups with her own heat. The pups cannot regulate their own temperature during the first few days of life.

WOLVES

FAMILY LIFE

Breeding takes place at any time in the winter months of January to April, but usually in February or March. In both North America and Eurasia mating takes place earlier among timber wolves than the tundra races farther north. The pups are born after a gestation period of 62 or 63 days. Four or five weeks before whelping, the pregnant alpha female will find a site for a den in which to give birth. This site may be determined partly by the usual location of prey within the pack's territory. In a large territory it is obviously an advantage if the pack hunters do not have to travel farther than necessary to bring food back to the hungry pups after making a kill. For this reason several dens may be dug by the alpha female and other pack members; some dens have been reported to be as much as 10 miles (16km) apart. The pups may be moved from one den to another before they are weaned.

Above and Below: Pups are born blind and deaf and with dark fur. These (Above) are about 10 days old, and beginning to open their eyes. They grow quickly and within a few weeks start to venture outside, staying close to their mother — as with these pups (Below) which are about three weeks old.

Right: At the entrance to the den a young pup licks her mother's muzzle to stimulate her to regurgitate food.

WOLVES

Suitable sites for a den are many and various: caves or holes in banks (which will be enlarged by the pregnant female); a natural stronghold such as a cavity formed under a pile of boulders or beneath a large fallen tree; or, especially in the far north, in eskers — river-formed ridges of sand, gravel and stones. In areas of sandy soil the female will often select a position on rising ground that will give a good view of the surrounding terrain from the den entrance. She will then excavate a large, gently sloping tunnel with an entrance no more than 24in (60cm) in diameter and anything from about 7–12ft (2.1–3.6m) long, which bends at the end to conclude in a cosy chamber that is invisible from the entrance.

Dens are usually sited near rivers, lakes or ponds: the nursing female requires a considerable daily intake of water. Timber wolves prefer to locate their dens in wooded areas to aid concealment. Alpha females often exhibit a preference for a particular type of vegetation; some may prefer spruce,

say, while others prefer cottonwood or particular kinds of shrubs. The same den may be used by an alpha female throughout her breeding life — that is, for four or five consecutive years; indeed, it may be used by a succession of alpha females within the same pack. This is obviously advantageous in the tundra, where permafrost makes it difficult to excavate a new den every year.

A typical litter will consist of four to six pups, but the number can vary widely from a single pup to nine or 10 (litters of up to 13 have been reported). The size of the litter will depend partly on the total number of wolves in the area, partly on the size of the pack, and partly on the abundance, or shortage, of prey animals in its territory.

Most of the litter will die before they are one year old. Some may be victims of hypothermia in an exceptionally cold spring; others may die from diseases such as distemper, or they may be killed (and eaten) by the adults because

WOLVES

they are crippled in some way, or they may be taken by a bear or lynx.

Newborn wolf pups are blind and deaf and have little sense of smell; and they are more or less incapable of regulating their own body temperature. They have dark fur, are pug-nosed and weigh about 1lb (450g). In favorable circum-stances the pups will grow rapidly, especially in their first three months of life, when they may put on 2lb (0.9kg) or more every week. Their mother keeps a scrupulously clean den: by licking the pups' bellies she can cause them to uri-nate or to produce faeces, which she removes by licking up.

The pups' eyes open when they are 11 to 15 days old, although their eyesight remains poor for another few weeks.

Below Left: Many pups begin to practise howling before the end of their first month.

Below: By eight weeks of age a dominance structure is emerging among mem-bers of the litter.

Their first teeth emerge at two weeks and a week later their sense of hearing begins to develop. Before they are a month old they are able to control their body temperature, and they start romping with their siblings around the entrance to the den. From now on they embark on a crash course of social-ization in which they forge emotional bonds and establish their dominance status with their litter-mates.

All the adult members of the pack manifest great interest in the pups, which lick their faces and solicit them to play. Such face licking is also the pups' way of begging for food, which will be regurgitated by an adult that has returned after taking part in a successful hunt. (Most observers believe that this food-begging method is in turn what might be called a rehearsal for what later will be very similar displays of submission behavior by subordinate adults.) Adults freely disgorge food when solicited by the pups. Often several adults will make piles of disgorged food. If the pups do not

want all the food, the adults will eat it again or cache it for consumption later. The partly digested food regurgitated by adults is in a semi-liquid state, enabling the mother wolf to begin a slow and gentle weaning process, which may be completed at any time between the pups' sixth and eighth weeks.

Pups will start to exhibit forms of predatory behavior soon after their first month. They may growl or snap at objects, and they will already have started to chew on twigs and anything available around the den. Once they have been weaned, the pups' upbringing and feeding is shared by all the adult members of the pack, some of whom will, for instance, look after the pups while their alpha female mother is out hunting with the rest of the pack. When the pups are about two months old they will be moved from the den to what are known as rendezvous sites — that is, areas in the territory, usually near water, where they will remain, often for several days, while the adults are hunting. The rendezvous sites are typically half an acre (0.2ha) or more in size, and will usually contain play areas and a resting area linked by trails.

What has been termed the "juvenile" period begins round about the third month and lasts until the pups attain sexual maturity at about 22 months. It is characterized by a gradual learning of the refinements of predatory behavior and hunting skills, and also by displays of aggressive behavior towards wolves belonging to other packs — an indication of the strengthening pack-oriented instincts of the pups. The pups' milk teeth are replaced at some time between their fourth and sixth month, and only then will the pups be equipped to hunt anything larger than rodents. By late autumn they will weigh 45–55lb (20–25kg) and are strong and swift enough to hunt: it is now that the learning process refines their instinctive predatory skills, so that by the turn of the year they will begin to play an active part in hunting down and killing moose, reindeer and other large prey. By the time the pups are a year old they have reached almost full size and may weigh 75–80lb (34–36kg). Some of them will be preparing to leave the pack and, ultimately, find a mate, mark out their own territory, and start a pack of their own.

Right: At two months, a pup's head, ears and paws seem to have outgrown the rest of its body.

Pages 94–95: Two pups compete in a tug-of-war for food.

Pages 96–97: Two captive adult wolves with a litter of pups.

WOLVES

WOLVES

HUNTING

The biologist L. David Mech, who has acquired an unrivaled knowledge of the North American gray wolf in field studies extending over more than 40 years, has noted with approval a proverb of northern Siberians: "The wolf is kept fed by its feet." The wolf is indeed an inveterate traveler in its never-ending quest for prey, often in rugged terrain in extremely hostile weather conditions. Its speed and sure-footedness over difficult ground or in snow is aided by the size of its feet: the footprint of a large timber wolf is more than 5in (127mm) long and 4.5in (114mm) wide. In motion the wolf habitually trots at about 5mph (8km/h) or lopes at about twice that speed. Its stamina is remarkable: when pursuing prey it can run at speeds of more than 20mph (32km/h) for up to a couple of miles; and individual wolves have been timed at more than 35mph (56km/h) over shorter distances.

After the birth of the pups in late March to early May the wolves' wanderings centre on the den or rendezvous site until late autumn. By then the surviving pups are old enough to accompany the rest of the pack on hunting expeditions, and the pack will usually need to travel farther afield in pursuit of the migrating herds of prey animals. In Alaska their main prey includes caribou, moose, and dall sheep; farther south, in Canada, it consists of big-horn sheep, moose, white-tailed deer, mule deer, and beaver; in Arctic and sub-arctic Eurasia the preferred prey are reindeer and elk; farther south the prey will include a variety of smaller ungulates. The size of a wolf pack's territory varies considerably, depending on a variety of factors, including the size of the pack, the abundance or shortage of prey animals, and the time of year (it is smaller in summer when the pups are confined to areas close to the rendezvous sites). Moreover, the boundaries of the territory may change quite frequently, especially in winter, when the pack is tracking the migrating caribou. The new boundaries will, of course, be marked by

Pages 98–99: In hot pursuit. The life of an adult wolf is dominated by the never-ending search for food: as soon as a prey carcass has been abandoned, the wolf is stimulated to return to the hunt.

Right: The North American bison or buffalo (*Bison bison*) is the largest of the gray wolf's prey animals, adult males weighing up to 2,000lb (900kg). Immense herds of these great beasts once roamed the vast plains of the United States and Canada east of the Rockies and were hunted relentlessly by packs of the now-extinct Great Plains subspecies of the gray wolf. Today, wolf-bison confrontations are rare except in areas such as Wood Buffalo National Park, Alberta.

WOLVES

Above: The caribou and its European equivalent, the reindeer (*Rangifer tarandus*), are the wolf's most important prey animals in the North American and Eurasian tundra and the great forests on its southern margin. In some regions wolf packs follow migrating herds of these ungulates for much of the year.

Right: Farther north, in the Canadian Arctic and northern Greenland, the musk-ox is a formidable prey animal. On the approach of wolves, a herd of musk-oxen forms into a tight circle, facing outwards, their heavy hooves and pointed horns offering a powerful challenge to the wolves' predatory skills.

fresh scent. And if, in the course of a hunt, a prey animal crosses a boundary into another pack's territory, the chasing pack may abandon the hunt and begin a search for alternative quarry. In winter packs in the Minnesota and Michigan national parks may have territories of about 150sq miles (390sq km), while those in Alaska and the Russian tundra may be up to 5,000sq miles (12,950sq km).

In general, wolves will hunt and attempt to kill suitable prey whenever their stomachs are empty. In the course of the winter they will travel huge distances, and whenever they are on the move they are hunting in the sense that they are actively looking for prey. They will not, however, invariably attack a prey animal when they have found it: a small pack, for instance, may hesitate to tackle a large bull moose in prime condition if it stands its ground. And even larger packs do not by any means always succeed in making a kill. It has been estimated that, on average, only about 10 per cent of attacks are successful among the smaller tundra packs, and wolves are accustomed, in lean times, to going for a fortnight between kills.

On their almost ceaseless winter travels, wolves will quite often chance upon an individual prey animal or even a herd. But most experts believe that they find their prey mainly by scent. If they are downwind if it, they may catch the scent at distances of up to a mile. When this happens, the leading wolf will stop and the whole pack will stand still for a moment, with noses pointing in the direction from which the scent signal comes. Sometimes they will then gather into a tight-

packed group, with tails wagging, almost as if they were collectively girding their loins before beginning their pursuit.

Another frequently used method of locating prey is by tracking — that is, by following the trail of hoof marks made by their quarry on the ground or in snow. Once the trail has been picked up, the wolves follow it eagerly, with noses to the ground. They follow the trail both visually and by scent — their sense of smell enabling them to confirm that the trail is freshly made (they will invariably ignore old track marks). The increasing freshness of the scent tells them that are getting closer to the prey even though it may not yet be visible to

them, and they gradually quicken their pace, their tails wagging with excitement. Evidently their aim at this stage is to get as close as possible without precipitating the prey's flight.

Finally, as the wolves approach, the prey becomes aware of them and may react in a variety of ways. Moose, elk, musk-oxen, even large deer, individually or collectively, may stand their ground. The wolves will usually then move closer, but with circumspection. An adult male moose may weigh up to 1,300lb (590kg), an elk up to 750lb (340kg), and a musk-ox up to 900lb (409kg); and each, if it stands and faces a wolf pack, will often, though by no means always, deter the wolves from attacking it. In general, wolves prefer to attack fleeing prey — with good reason: when in flight a moose, for instance, has much less chance to bring its most effective defensive armoury — its forefeet and antlers — to bear on its attackers. Once the wolves are within, say, 100ft (30m) of their prey, their aim is to make it flee. If they succeed they chase it at full speed: indeed, they seem to need the stimulus of a bolting prey to make them press home the attack.

Right: A juvenile bighorn sheep (*Ovis canadensis*) in Jasper National Park, western Alberta. Wolves try to attack bighorns from above, driving their quarry onto lower, flatter terrain.

Below: The moose (*Alces alces*) and its Eurasian cousin the elk are the gray wolf's largest antlered prey, the males weighing up to 1,300lb (590kg).

Pages 106–107: After a kill the alpha male and female usually get the first chance to feed. Here a subordinate pack member (on the left) shows submissive behavior to encourage the feasting pair to allow him access to the carcass.

WOLVES

They may chase their quarry for several miles, but this is rare. On many occasions a pack will chase prey only a short distance — less than half a mile — before giving up. Indeed, if it does not gain significantly on its quarry in the first few seconds of the chase, there seems to be a collective acknowledgement that pursuit is useless — either the prey is too large or too fast, or the terrain is unsuitable for an attack.

If it encounters a herd of potential prey, whether moose, caribou, elk or deer, the pack leader will select the most vulnerable individual — often a calf or an injured or otherwise infirm older animal — and will try to separate it from the rest of the herd. This can sometimes be achieved simply by forcing the herd to flee at a speed too great for all its members to maintain. A female moose will fiercely defend its calf, but the calf will usually succumb if the pack persists in its attack.

If the pack succeeds in overtaking a large prey animal, the leading wolves will usually attack its rump, where they are less vulnerable to potentially lethal blows from the quarry's hind hooves. If they manage to halt the prey, one or more wolves will attempt to seize it by the nose, while others attack its throat, neck, sides, and other areas. If an exceptionally strong animal manages to shake off such an attack, a pack will sometimes call off the engagement for a few hours, or even a day, until the wounded prey is weakened by loss of blood. Usually, if half a dozen or more wolves manage to take hold of the prey, it will be dead within a few minutes.

The wolves then gorge on the dead animal, the alpha members having choice of site (usually the abdomen) and the others piling in to grab what they can. If the prey is large, each member of the pack will eat anything up to 20lb (9kg) of meat. They may then dig holes some distance away and cache more meat, either taken from the carcass or regurgitated from their own stomachs, for future consumption.

The gray wolf is an intelligent animal and one that has adapted to survival in exceptionally harsh environments. Its method of hunting co-operatively — one of the reasons why some people fear and hate it — is but one aspect of what is a rich and complex social life that is unique among members of the genus Canis. Although it has been hunted or poisoned to extinction in most of the United States except Alaska, and although its limited populations in parts of eastern Europe and Russia are still hunted for what some people choose to call sport, it must be hoped that more enlightened attitudes towards potentially endangered species in general will enable this remarkable beast to survive, at least in the great Holarctic wildernesses.

Below: Even when most of the prey's flesh has been eaten a wolf will often chew on the bones, its powerful jaws making short work of a skeleton.

Right: Except in times of extreme food shortage, members of a wolf pack will allow every member of a hunt to eat its fill.

Pages 110–111: The chase: once the prey is within striking range, the pack surges forward in pursuit.

WOLVES

The Gray Wolf's Cousins

THE GRAY WOLF'S COUSINS

COYOTE (*Canis latrans*)

The coyote is also known as the brush wolf or prairie wolf — names that do little justice to its remarkable range of habitats, from burning deserts to the tundra and the margins of the great northern forests. The name coyote comes from a Spanish corruption of the Aztec *coyotl*, which means "barking dog"; its specific name derives from the Latin *latro*=to bark. The coyote is a New World species and is confined to North America and northern parts of Central America (its Old World "equivalents" are the jackals).

The coyote's range at the time of the early European colonization of North America was essentially to the west of the Mississippi river: it was found from Alaska (where its ancestors had originally entered the New World from Eurasia) to Costa Rica. Its spread eastward was for long restricted by the gray wolf, which even today will prey on the coyote where their ranges overlap. The 20th century eradication campaign, as we have seen, has wiped out the gray wolf from almost all of the United States except Alaska; and this has enabled the coyote (the other chief target of the campaign) to colonize the whole of the United States as well as most of the southern half of Canada. Coyotes are found not only in the wilderness: they have invaded the suburbs of many of the great cities, including Chicago, Los Angeles, New York, Kansas City, and Houston (Texas), where they raid rubbish dumps and steal food left out for pets on back doorsteps — rather in the way the red fox has adapted to city life in Britain.

Coyotes superficially look very much like small gray wolves. A close examination of a wolf and a coyote of the same size, however, reveals a number of differences. The coyote has a relatively larger brain case and a more slender, rather fox-like muzzle; and its ears are proportionately considerably larger than the wolf's. The coyote's pelage is buff or grayish-buff on the head, neck and back, and on some individuals the coats have black ticking; the fur on the underparts and the inside of the legs is invariably paler in color.

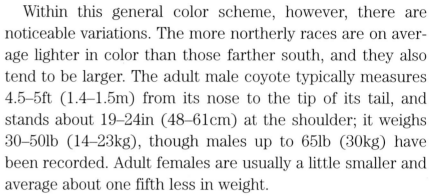

Within this general color scheme, however, there are noticeable variations. The more northerly races are on average lighter in color than those farther south, and they also tend to be larger. The adult male coyote typically measures 4.5–5ft (1.4–1.5m) from its nose to the tip of its tail, and stands about 19–24in (48–61cm) at the shoulder; it weighs 30–50lb (14–23kg), though males up to 65lb (30kg) have been recorded. Adult females are usually a little smaller and average about one fifth less in weight.

The coyote is not a pack animal like the gray wolf, but a mated pair will usually remain together for several years. Mating takes place in January or February, after the female has undergone a long pre-oestrus period of 10 to 12 weeks. The gestation period averages 63 days, during which time the female makes a den or enlarges the abandoned burrow of another animal, such as a badger, or another coyote; she may use the same den for several years. Like the gray wolf, the coyote favors a den site near a river or pond. The average litter is five or six pups. The mother nurses her pups for the first three weeks of life, after which she and her mate provide them with regurgitated food. Before they are two months old their parents will start to bring them freshly killed rodents, rabbits and other prey.

The young usually remain with their parents for their first year, although the family will as a rule break up into groups of two or at most three to hunt for food. The coyote's diet is more varied than that of almost every other carnivore. The most important food items are rodents and other small mammals, including ground squirrels, gophers, hares, rabbits, and mice; but they also eat birds, reptiles (including rattlesnakes), insects, and even fish, as well as fruits and

Pages 112–113: A pair of black-backed jackals, members of the southern race of this species, greet each other on the edge of the Namibian Desert to the east of Cape Cross. Here they scavenge along the coast or occasionally seize fur-seal pups.

Right: The coyote, once confined mainly to the southwestern United States, colonized most of the country following the virtual eradication of the gray wolf, and it has also penetrated most of subarctic Canada.

WOLVES

herbaceous plants. Ungulates that feature in their diet include elk and deer; but these will usually be lame or otherwise weakened individuals or their young; or they may have been scavenged as carrion.

Although a mated pair will sometimes hunt together, especially in search of larger prey, the coyote is mainly a solitary hunter. Remarkably, however, coyotes sometimes "co-operate" with badgers in hunting burrowing animals such as rabbits and ground squirrels. A coyote will remain by one of the burrow entrances while the badger digs away at another part of the burrow. When the prey dashes out of the excavated burrow, whichever predator is closer to it will get the prize. It is not genuine co-operation, of course; but the coyote and badger are not natural enemies, and both benefit from these temporary partnerships, which have been observed (and photographed) on many occasions.

The American Indians called the coyote the song dog, with good reason. It howls, mainly at dusk, all the year round but most frequently during autumn and winter. The sound is higher pitched than that of the gray wolf and consists mainly of a series of short notes rather than the long single note of the wolf. The coyote's howl seems to serve the same purposes as that of the wolf's.

For more than 150 years, and especially since the first decade of the 20th century, it has been subjected to a concerted and relentless eradication campaign by U.S. government agencies, stock-farmers and other interests. The essential folly of this campaign was highlighted in the early 1960s by a parallel campaign launched by the U.S. Department of Agriculture in which hundreds of tons of poi-

Above: The coyote's range in the United States covers a wide climatic spectrum. Here it leaves its characteristic footprint in a dry river bed in the southwest.

Right: It is equally at home in the snows of Canada and Alaska. All over its range its diet is composed mainly of small mammals — hares, gophers, ground squirrels, mice — together with any birds, reptiles and insects they can catch and even windfalls such as fruit.

WOLVES

sons and gas cartridges were laid over three million acres (1.2 million ha) of public and private land in an attempt to wipe out rodents such as ground squirrels, hares, prairie dogs, gophers and others that were stripping bare huge areas of pasture grazed by cattle and sheep. The war against the coyote was ostensibly intended to deny it its modest annual toll of cattle and, more particularly, sheep. If the U.S. Department of Agriculture had spent a little more time researching the problem, they would have discovered that the rodent plague was substantially attributable to the campaign against the coyotes, which if left to themselves would have kept the pests under control.

The coyote has its own ways of dealing with the eradication campaign. It has not only become much more resourceful in evading the attentions of the farmers and government hunters; to compensate for its losses, in many areas it is now breeding earlier in the year and producing larger litters. It is the supreme survivor among the New World canids.

RED WOLF (*Canis rufus*)

In bleak contrast to the prosperity of the coyote, the red wolf is on the very cusp of extinction. Moreover, many biologists

Pages 118–119: A coyote pup rubs its muzzle against a log, attracted by a scent mark that has been made by an adult.

Left: A captive red wolf. In appearance and size the species comes midway between the eastern gray wolf and the coyote.

Below: A formerly captive red wolf in the Great Smoky Mountains National Park, Tennessee. This region was once part of the range of the large eastern subspecies, closest in kin to the gray wolf.

Above: A captive-bred red wolf released into Great Smoky Mountains N.P. wears a radio-location collar so that its movements can be monitored.

Left: Penned red wolves at the captive-breeding center in Great Smoky Mountains N.P.

Pages 124–125: A penned red wolf at the breeding center provides a seat for its companion.

have voiced doubts about its authenticity as a distinct species, suggesting that it may in fact be a hybrid between its closest kin, the gray wolf and the coyote, and recent genetic research seems to support this. At all events the wolf known as *Canis rufus* closely resembles a somewhat longer-legged coyote in general appearance — it stands 24–30in (60–76cm) at the shoulders — but it has a darker, often distinctly reddish pelage sometimes touched with dark grey or black. Its weight, typically 35–65lb (16–30kg), is midway

between that of the coyote and gray wolf, as is the pitch of its howling.

Its original range extended over much of the southeastern United States, from central Texas in the west to Florida in the east and from the Gulf of Mexico in the south to southern Missouri and Indiana in the north. Typical habitats included deciduous and evergreen forests, coastal plains, and wetlands abutting the eastern seaboard and the Gulf; the hot and humid climate of such wetlands is atypical of the habitats of true coyotes. The red wolf also differed from the coyote in that it frequently hunted in groups of three or four, such groups being capable of killing ungulates such as white-tailed deer and at least disabling cattle.

Three subspecies have been recognized. The largest and darkest-colored red wolves, *Canis rufus floridanus*, were those in the eastern part of its range; a somewhat smaller subspecies, *C. r. gregoryi*, was found farther west, in the Mississippi valley; and a still smaller subspecies, *C. r. rufus*, with a noticeably more tawny or buff-colored coat, occurred mainly in Texas. This and other factors has led to the belief among some taxonomists that the red wolf is indeed a cross between the eastern gray wolf, *Canis lupus lycaon*, which was once the dominant canid in this region, and an eastern subspecies of the coyote, *Canis latrans frustror*, with the eastern red wolves most strongly resembling the eastern gray wolf and the western ones more similar to the coyote. The regional variations would be accounted for by further hybridization between the local red wolf population and the gray wolf or coyote.

By the early 1970s red wolves had become virtually extinct throughout their ancestral range. The process of extinction was triggered at least in part by habitat destruction and persecution by man and also by parasitic diseases, and it was accelerated by increasing hybridization, especially with coyotes, which further undermined the genetic integrity of the original populations. The red wolf was accorded endangered status by the U.S. Department of Agriculture in 1967, and in 1973 a breeding program was launched using the few captured red wolves which, after careful examinations, including skull X-rays, were declared to be "true" reds, rather than coyotes or hybrids.

In 1988 eight red wolves from the breeding program's total of 130 were released into the Alligator River National Wildlife

WOLVES

Refuge, in North Carolina, where the local wildlife includes rabbits, raccoons, opossums, muskrats, and wild turkeys and other red wolf prey. A little later others were released into the Great Smoky Mountains National Park, south of Knoxville, Tennessee. These projects give at least some hope of the red wolf's survival, although it seems probable that the lack of genetic diversity among the breeding stock may cause problems that may well be compounded by further hybridisation with local coyotes.

JACKALS

The jackals are the Old World equivalents, and indeed the closest relatives, of the coyote, evolving as they did from the same ancestral canid that originally arose in Eurasia some two to three million years ago. They migrated south and west and today are found mainly in Africa and the Middle East; the ranges of all three species overlap in parts of East Africa. The jackals are superficially similar in appearance to the coyote, although they are significantly smaller than their North American cousin.

Golden Jackal (*Canis aureus*)

The golden jackal is also known as the Asiatic, the Indian, the yellow, the silver-backed, and the common jackal — the number and variety of its common names reflecting the size of its range. It is found right across northern Africa from Mauritania to Ethiopia and as far south as Tanzania; in the Balkans (where, as we have seen, it has replaced the gray wolf in parts of Bulgaria); in Turkey and Armenia, the Middle East, the Indian subcontinent, and Burma and Thailand.

Unsurprisingly in view of its vast range, more than a dozen races of golden jackal have been proposed, their differences mainly concerning size, the length and color of pelage, and slight variations in dentition. An adult male measures 15–20in (38–51cm) at the shoulder and weighs 15–28lb (7–13kg); the females are considerably smaller. The color and length of the pelage varies according to their habitat: desert-dwelling jackals tend to have a lighter-colored and shorter coat than those living elsewhere. It is typically grayish-yellow, sometimes with a reddish tinge, especially on the legs. The guard hairs along the back are often black at the tips. The muzzle and ears are usually buff-colored, while the underparts and insides of the legs are pale grey or whitish.

The golden jackal has accommodated itself to a variety of habitats, from mountain regions up to an altitude of about 13,000ft (3,950m) to arid semi-desert (though it is rarely found in true desert except around oases), from woodland and forest to riverine marshland, and from the environs of human settlements to open savanna, such as Tanzania's Serengeti National Park.

Although they are expert scavengers of carrion, they also hunt rodents, rabbits and hares, ground-dwelling birds (including domestic poultry), insects, and fish. Insects form an important part of their diet, especially locusts and dung beetles. In the Serengeti, mated pairs of golden jackals prey successfully on Thomson's gazelles, especially during the fawning season from January to May, when the young are taken in large numbers to help feed the jackal pups, which average three to five in a litter.

Pages 126–127: The distinctive pelage of the black-backed jackal has given rise to a variety of other common names, including silver-backed and saddleback.

Right: A black-backed jackal in Kenya's Masai Mara Game Reserve. The local Swahili name for the species in this region is *bweha* — an imitation of the sound of its commonest vocal call.

Below: A side-striped jackal displays the characteristic stripe of pale fur running along its flanks. This one is hunting in the Moremi Game Reserve on the northern edge of Botswana's Okavango Delta.

WOLVES

Above: A black-backed jackal searches for prey on the Kenya savanna. Essentially solitary, this species sometimes hunts in pairs to prey on gazelles or even new-born wildebeest.

Right: A pair of three-month-old black-backed jackals resting outside their den. There may be anything up to eight pups in a litter, though fewer than half are likely to survive.

Pages 132–133: When searching for food the black-backed jackal may travel anything up to 30 miles (48km) in a night, keeping up a steady trot for miles on end. If it cannot find live prey, it will follow lions or hyenas on their hunts, scavenging whatever these larger predators leave.

The golden jackal's howl typically consists of a long, ascending wail repeated several times, followed by two or three short yips. It will often elicit a similar response from neighboring jackals. Its vocal response to humans or to a larger predator is a sharp bark or yelp.

WOLVES

Side-striped Jackal (*Canis adustus*)

This is the largest of the jackals, standing 20–22in (51–56cm) at the shoulder and weighing up to 30lb (13.5kg). It is more wolf-like in general appearance than the other jackals both in its typically lupine short and broad muzzle and in the texture of its coat. It takes its common name from the line of guard hairs, running along its sides from the shoulder to the base of the tail, that is a noticeably paler color than the rest of the pelage, which is brownish-gray on the back and flanks and a somewhat lighter color on the chest, underparts, and legs.

Its range extends in the north from Senegal and Nigeria eastwards to Ethiopia and southern Sudan, and in the south from Angola and northern Namibia right across central Africa to Kenya in the north down to Transvaal and Natal provinces in South Africa. Its diet consists of rodents and other small mammals, birds, and birds' eggs, reptiles, invertebrates, and also any carrion that it can find; in the southern part of its range it also includes a considerable intake of fruits and vegetables. Breeding takes place at different times of the year: in equatorial parts of its range there is little seasonal change in temperature or length of day. In southern parts of its range it breeds in winter (July). The gestation period of up to 70 days is longer than that of most other canids, and a litter will typically consist of three or four pups.

Right: A black-backed jackal quenches its thirst at a waterhole near Savuti, in Chobe National Park, northern Botswana.

Below: A young black-backed jackal with adult pelage. Note the red tinge of its lower side and outer surfaces of the legs, and its bushy, black-tipped tail.

WOLVES

Unlike the golden jackal, the side-striped does not howl and is, in general, more taciturn than the other two species. It occasionally gives vent to a series of low-pitched single barks, but its habitual silence is in keeping with its shyness: rarely seen by man, its preferred habitat is dense woods or bush, preferably near water.

Black-backed Jackal (*Canis mesomelas*)

Also known as the silver-backed or saddleback jackal, this species' most distinctive identifying feature is the saddle-shaped area of mixed black and silvery white guard hairs on the neck and back. The area, darker in some individuals than in others, is widest across the shoulders and tapers to a point at the base of the tail. The sides of head and body and outer sides of the legs are light reddish-brown, and the underparts of the body are creamy beige. The brown tail has a black tip.

There are two quite separate African populations. The northern extends from Somalia and central Ethiopia southward through Uganda and Kenya and into Tanzania and eastern Zambia. The southern population is found in southern Angola, Namibia, Botswana, Zimbabwe, southern Mozambique, and throughout South Africa. In contrast to its shyer side-striped cousin, with which it shares parts of its range, the black-backed jackal favors relatively open terrain, including even the savanna, where it often tracks hunting lions and cheetahs, and waits to feed on the remains of ungulate carcasses abandoned by the big cats.

The black-backed jackal also hunts in its own right, and mated pairs and larger groups prey on Thomson's and other gazelles and on the young of larger ungulates. In its southern range, where large areas have been cleared of their natural prey for farming, black-backed jackals frequently kill sheep, especially lambs during the breeding season. The hunting groups consist of a mated pair, any of their young that are old enough to hunt, and may also include one or more non-breeding adults who act as helpers.

There are usually three or four pups to a litter. The pups are ready to hunt at about three months of age, and some will

Right: A pair of young black-backed jackals at play in the arid scrubland of Moremi Game Reserve.

Pages 138–139: Adept scavengers, black-backed jackals often rely for food on the remains of prey killed by much larger animals. This one feeds on a wildebeest carcass abandoned by lions in Kenya's Masai Mara.

WOLVES

leave the family group well before the end of their first year. This species, like the other jackals, has many natural enemies apart from man. In some areas they are a favored prey of leopards. Pythons are also known to kill them, and many fall victim to large birds of prey and to baboons.

ETHIOPIAN WOLF (*Canis simensis*)

This species, which is found only in Ethiopia, is the least known member of the genus *Canis* — a fact attested to by

Pages 140–141: An Ethiopian wolf asleep on moorland high in the Balé Mountains National Park in central Ethiopia. The Balé race of wolf is somewhat larger and more reddish in color than the northern race in the Simien mountains.

Below: Somewhat resembling a large fox in general appearance, the Ethiopian wolf has more in common with jackals than with other wolves.

Right: An Ethiopian wolf with four pups, two of which are soliciting her to regurgitate food. Litters range in size from three to seven pups.

its proliferation of somewhat confusing common names: it is also known as the Ethiopian red fox, red jackal, Simien fox, and Simien jackal. The last two common names, and its specific name, come from the Simien mountains in northern Ethiopia, its most northerly range; its other ranges include upland areas of Shewa province, north of Addis Ababa; and, farther south, the Arusi mountains and the Balé Mountains National Park. In all these ranges, its most typical habitats are high-plateau moorlands at altitudes between 9,500ft and 16,000ft (2,750m–4,875m) above sea level.

Taxonomically, the species unquestionably belongs to the genus *Canis* as opposed to the Old World fox genus *Vulpes*, but it has more in common with the jackals than with true wolves. Its skull is similar in shape to a jackal's, but it has a longer, somewhat fox-like muzzle. The adult male stands 20–24in (51–61cm) at the shoulder, is notably long in the leg, and weighs 35–40lb (16–18kg); the female is a little smaller. The pelage is distinctly red in color along the back, sides, upper chest and legs; underparts, lower chest and about half the length of the tail are light buff or white, and the remainder of the tail to its tip is black. The Simien plateau race is slightly lighter in colour than the races farther south.

The Ethiopian wolf preys mainly on rabbits and hares and a variety of rodents, notably the giant mole rat. It is a solitary hunter, although naturally gregarious. Sexually mature wolves pair in the autumn and mate during the winter, up to seven pups being born after a 65- to 68-day gestation.

It is estimated that there are several hundred Ethiopian wolves in Balé Mountains National Park, where they are protected. Elsewhere they are hunted by farmers, who claim (erroneously) that the wolf preys on sheep, and by others who value their pelts. Their survival in the wild is problematic: they are among the most endangered species of wild canid.

DINGO (*Canis familiaris dingo*)

The origins and evolutionary history of the dingo of Australia have long been matters of speculation among biologists. It seems certain that it was introduced into Australia by the descendants of the first human settlers, who had arrived from the north — probably from or via New Guinea — between 40,000 and 50,000 years ago. But there is no evidence of the presence of the dingo on the continent until 4,000 to 8,000 years ago, which is some time after man first domesticated

the dog. It was at one time assumed that the Aborigines who had introduced it had also domesticated it, presumably as a hunting dog as well as a pet. In fact, neither the Aborigines nor anyone else (including experienced Australian police dog-trainers) has succeeded in inducing submission behavior, let alone obedience, in the dingo, although it will sometimes show apparent affection for humans.

The dingo is found in most of the vast central desert areas of Australia, the Nullarbor Plain in the south, the northern regions from the Hamersley Range in Western Australia eastward to Cape York Peninsula in Queensland, and down most of the eastern coast; it is absent from Tasmania. The dingo's pelage varies from region to region. On the Nullarbor Plain it is pale beige and white; yellowish-brown in the west-central Gibson Desert; gingery red in the mountains in the southeast; rust red in Arnhem Land and elsewhere in the far north; and black or brindle individuals are found in various regions. Any of these may have white areas on the chest, feet and tip of the tail. Dingoes can vary considerably in size and weight: adult males may measure 15–26in (38–66cm) at the shoulder and weigh 40–70lb (18–32kg); the largest individuals are found in the eastern parts of their range.

Dingoes breed in the winter and their pups are born in the early spring. The newborn pups are black, with white tips to their tails. Dingoes will also readily mate with domestic dogs, and the resultant hybrids will interbreed with other hybrids or with dingoes or dogs. True dingoes have noticeably larger canine and carnassial teeth than hybrids or domestic dogs of similar size. They prey on a wide variety of animals, including rodents and rabbits, but their preference is for kangaroos and wallabies — and sheep. They have been hunted, shot and poisoned in their hundreds of thousands since the mid-19th century for their predation of sheep, but the only effective countermeasure has been the erection of specially designed dingo fences in sheep-grazing areas.

Pages 144–145: A two-month-old Ethiopian wolf pup at play outside its den. The pups are reared in underground dens that are often dug into banks or the base of cliffs and have more than one entrance.

Right: The Ethiopian wolf's survival is threatened by farmers, by hunters who value their pelts, and by dogs who compete with the wolves in hunting for hares, rodents, and other prey animals.

Five Other Wild Canids

FIVE OTHER WILD CANIDS

This chapter briefly considers five wild canids which are distantly related to the gray wolf, but show something of the varieties of size and form within the family Canidae. The five chosen range from the maned wolf, which in fact is not a wolf at all, through the otter-like bush dog and raccoon-like raccoon dog, to two species of wild dog which, although unlike the wolf in appearance, have much in common with it in terms of behavior and social organization. Two of the species are from South America, two from Asia, and one from Africa.

MANED WOLF (*Chrysocyon brachyurus*)

The maned wolf is believed to have a more ancient evolutionary history than any other South American canid. Unique as it is, it nevertheless is more closely related to the New World foxes (*Dusicyon*) than to any species of the genus *Canis*. Its present range extends southward from the southern margins of the Amazon rain forest in Brazil, through the Mato Grosso with its open woodlands and grassy plains, and on to Paraguay, parts of Uruguay, and northern Argentina; in the west its range includes parts of eastern Bolivia.

Physically the maned wolf is distinguished mainly by its exceptionally long, stilt-like legs, giving it a height of 28–30in (71–76cm) at the shoulder. The adult male weighs 40–45lb (18–20kg). Apart from its legs, it looks much more like a fox than like a wolf, with its long, pointed snout and large, pointed ears and long, somewhat shaggy coat. The coat is generally chestnut red and is especially luxuriant about the neck and shoulders (whence its common name); the part of the "mane" immediately behind the ears and extending a short way along the back is usually darker, even black, as are the legs and part of the muzzle; the end half of the relatively short tail is cream or white.

Maned wolves have large territories and they are solitary hunters. Although they are meat-eaters by choice, they are omnivorous in their diet. Small rodents and, when they can catch them, birds are their main prey and they also eat considerable quantities of vegetables and fruit. Those living near human settlements also prey on domestic poultry, which has led to their being hunted by farmers, many of whom believe, mistakenly, that maned wolves also prey on sheep. Their pelts have no commercial value as they have little or no undercoat.

A pared male and female mate some time between January and June. In spite of the long breeding season, however, the female remains on heat for only five days. The gestation period of about 65 days is fractionally longer than the average for canids. The female rarely gives birth to more than three pups; these are darker and somewhat grayer in color than the adults for their first few days, and their legs are noticeably shorter in proportion to their overall size. After weaning they are fed by both their parents, first with regurgitated food and later with kills. The young reach sexual maturity at about 18 months of age.

In Uruguay and Bolivia the maned wolf's prospects of survival are poor; they may, indeed, be extinct in both countries by now. In Argentina and Paraguay there are probably 1,000 to 1,500, mainly in the extreme north. In Brazil there may be 3,000 or more, and the numbers may be rising in areas where forests are being cleared to make way for grasslands.

SOUTH AMERICAN BUSH DOG (*Speothos venaticus*)

The distinctive appearance of this canid, known locally by its Spanish name, *zorro vinagre* (vinegar fox), seems to have more in common with that of an otter than that of a fox or a wolf. The adult male is 24–26in (61–66cm) long, excluding the tail, but is only 10–12in (25–30cm) tall at the shoulder;

Pages 148–149: A pack of African wild dogs attacking a wildebeest in the Serengeti National Park, northwestern Tanzania.

Right: The maned wolf is not a wolf at all but a unique species of canid related to foxes. Its large ears, pointed snout and red pelage are distinctly foxlike.

Page 152: A maned wolf in hot pursuit of prey in Brazil's Mato Grosso.

Page 153: The maned wolf is omnivorous, eating anything from small rodents, birds, and domestic poultry to a variety of fruits.

WOLVES

its well-furred tail is only 5–6in (13–15cm) in length. Its head has a short muzzle and short, round ears set well apart. Its coat is short and mid- to dark brown in color, and, unlike that of most canids, is darker on the underparts than elsewhere.

The bush dog's range extends from the easternmost parts of Panama to most parts of South America east of the Andes as far as northern Argentina and Paraguay. Although the range is enormous, the bush dog population is nowhere very large. The dog prefers fairly open country, where grasslands begin to give way to forest, and they invariably live close to water. They usually live in family groups in which there are clear dominance hierarchies. They make their burrows by excavating holes in the ground; sometimes they take over dens dug by armadilloes or other animals. The adult females are believed to have more than one period of oestrus a year; the gestation period is 64–70 days and a litter typically contains three or four pups.

The bush dog is an exceptionally capable swimmer, under water as well as at the surface. This makes it a formidable hunter of its preferred prey, the capybara and the paca, both of which are large, essentially aquatic rodents. Bush dogs hunt in packs and are said to be capable of bringing down animals as large as deer.

South American Indians sometimes keep bush dogs as pets. The animals seem to exhibit the intelligence and behavior patterns of domestic dogs and the young in particular respond to petting with squeaks and excited tail wagging. Their vocal repertoire also includes a variety of barks and high-pitched sounds resembling bird calls. The bush dog appears to have no natural enemies in the wild and, although nowhere abundant, seems to be in no danger of extinction.

RACCOON DOG (*Nyctereutes procyonoides*)

This species' common and specific names are apt: with its short, sturdy legs, apparently stout body, and unusual coat markings, it bears more than a passing resemblance to the raccoon (*Procyon*). Like the raccoon, its winter coat, especially in its most northerly ranges, is luxuriant, with the guard hairs particularly long and thick over the rump, the belly, the sides of the head, and the tail. The coat is blackish with brown or pale cream splashes or streaks. The darkest areas of pelage are the lower half of the face, the throat and chest, and the legs and underparts.

The raccoon dog is a native of Japan, China, Mongolia, south-eastern Siberia, northern Vietnam and Cambodia. In the late 1920s and 1930s it was deliberately introduced into the Soviet Union with the intention of exploiting the commercial value of its pelt. It has since spread westward through much of eastern Europe, Scandinavia and Germany, and by the 1980s it had reached France.

It is found mainly in wooded areas (though rarely in evergreen forest) and other places that provide dense natural cover, preferably near water. Its varied diet consists of rodents and other small mammals, lizards, frogs and toads (it is a capable swimmer), ground-dwelling birds and invertebrates, as well as fruits, berries and other vegetable matter. It hunts mainly at night, spending most of the day in a burrow (often one abandoned by a fox).

The adult male raccoon dog typically measures 25–35in (64-89cm) in length including its 7–10in (18–25cm) long tail; it stands 12–15in (31–38cm) at the shoulder. Its weight varies considerably at different times of the year: in spring and summer it is 8–13lb (3.5–6kg), but with the onset of autumn it steadily puts on weight until by the end of November it will weigh 14–24lb (6.5–11kg). It then retires to its burrow for the winter, which is spent in semi-hibernation. If, however, the weather is mild it may emerge and begin winter feeding; this often happens in the southerly parts of their range.

The winter sleep may end, depending on location in the range, at any time between late February and April. The dogs pair up and mate soon after they emerge (mated pairs usually remain together for life). The pups, typically five to a litter, are born after a gestation period of 60–63 days. The male provides food for its mate and then, when they are weaned, for the pups. Raccoon dogs do not seem to have a strong territorial instinct, and often several mated pairs will live in dens located within a few yards of each other. The young are sexually mature by the end of their first year. They rarely live longer than three or four years.

Right: The raccoon dog, unlike most other canids, is a creature of Eurasian woodland areas, especially deciduous forest, and in northern parts of their range they hibernate during the winter.

DHOLE (*Cuon alpinus*)

Also known as the Asiatic wild dog or whistling dog, the dhole once inhabited much of Eurasia south of the Arctic regions. Today, however, it has been eliminated from Europe. Its present range extends eastwards from the Pamir foothills, through southern Siberia, Xinjiang (Sinkiang), Tibet, the Indian subcontinent (but not Sri Lanka), and Burma, Mongolia, most of China apart from the northeast, and the Indo-Chinese peninsula as far south and east as Sumatra and Java. Its habitats vary greatly, from open steppes in Mongolia to dense tropical and subtropical forests and jungles in the southern parts of its range.

Similar in appearance to the Indian pariah dog or to some domestic mongrels, the dhole stands anything from 16in to 22in (40–56cm) and weighs 38lb to 46lb (17–21kg), the largest individuals being found in the northern populations. The coat colors also vary depending on geographical location: the southern dholes are predominantly a rusty red in color; those further north are more of a greyish brown, while pale beige-colored individuals also occur. The guard hairs along the spine may be black-tipped, and in some individuals the bushy tail is wholly black, as are the tips of the cocked, rounded ears. Northern dholes have longer guard hairs and a denser undercoat than their southern relatives. The dhole has a short, square muzzle, somewhat convex in profile. Its dentition is unique among the canids in that the lower jaw has only two molars, rather than the usual three, on each side.

Dholes live in packs, typically of 8 to 12 individuals, most of them related. On occasions outside the breeding period a number of packs will temporarily combine to form what are called clans of anything from 35 to 70 or more individuals. There is a clear dominance hierarchy within each pack. The young are born, after a gestation period of 60–62 days, in January or February in the south and in February to April in northern parts of the range.

Dholes hunt mainly in packs and are capable of killing large prey, such as reindeer in Siberia and young buffalo in India. Their main prey in the south, however, are antelope

Right: Aptly named, the raccoon dog resembles the unrelated raccoon (*Procyon lotor*) of North America, with its short legs and stout body and characteristic markings of the facial fur.

WOLVES

and deer, especially the chital or spotted deer (*Axis*); they also hunt the larger sambhur and swamp deer, the nilgal antelope, wild pigs, wild and domestic sheep and goats, and even langur monkeys. The dhole can howl, snarl, whine and bark, though the last is little more than a rapid series of yaps. Its commonest vocal sound, however, is a sort of hissing whistle, which hunters have learned to imitate in order to attract dholes within range of their guns.

AFRICAN WILD DOG (*Lycaon pictus*)

This species, sometimes called the African, or Cape, hunting dog, once ranged over almost the whole of the African continent south of the southern fringes of the Sahara desert. Today its range has shrunk to central parts of the countries on the Gulf of Guinea, southern Sudan, Ethiopia, Somalia, parts of Kenya (including the Masai Mara), Tanzania (including the Serengeti), and all of southern Africa as far south as northern Transvaal. In all these regions its preferred habitats are savanna grassland, arid bush and open woodland.

The African wild dog's appearance is quite unlike that of any other wild canid. The young animal's coat has a basically white background color with randomly shaped black areas; as it matures, its coat acquires light brown or yellowish markings that compound an already somewhat blotchy appearance. The shapes and colors of the markings vary radically from one individual to the next. The coat is short except on the lower throat and chest and on the bushy tail, which often is white-tipped. The unusually large, oval-shaped ears are normally held erect. A curious anatomical feature is the absence of a dew claw on the front feet. Largest of the wild canids of Africa, it stands 28–32in (71–81cm) at the shoulder and may weigh 56lb (25kg) or more.

The most highly social of all canids apart from the gray wolf, the African wild dog lives in packs that vary in size between 6 and 18 or more individuals, depending partly upon habitat and the general availability of prey. For most of the year, apart from the breeding period, they are highly nomadic, ranging over hunting areas that may be as large as 600sq miles (1,550sq km).

Unlike the wolf pack, that of the wild dog consists of mostly related adult males and yearlings led by a dominant female usually of a different lineage, who will breed with one (or sometimes more) of the males. The mating period is not confined to one particular season and pups may be born at almost any time of the year. In parts of the wild dog's range, however, it is noticeable that more pups are born during the dry season, when the principal prey animals are easier to hunt because they remain within easy reach of the few water holes that have not dried up.

The breeding female may have 12 or more pups. The social structure of the pack is validated, so to speak, by the curious fact that she invariably has more male than female pups. The females will usually leave the pack at 18 months of age or a little later, some eventually to form a pack of their own. All adults and yearlings help to feed and look after the pups until the latter are old enough to join the hunt.

The pack hunts in the morning and in the early evening. Its prey varies from region to region but typically consists of ungulates such as wildebeest, kudu, impala, and Grant's and Thomson's gazelles; in addition young buffalo and zebras will also be taken. The wild dog pack is a formidably efficient hunting machine with a kill rate far higher than that of other canids or of the big cats with whom it competes for food in many parts of its range. The pack will chase fleeing prey for several miles and can sustain speeds of 30mph (48km/h) and more for minutes on end. The ferocity of their assault on their prey contrasts strikingly with their behavior once it has been killed, when the youngest members of the hunting group are often allowed to eat first.

The African wild dog has been ruthlessly hunted by man throughout its range. Some 50 years ago pack sizes were considerably larger than today's, often consisting of as many as 35 or more individuals, and multiple-pack gatherings of several hundred could often be observed in the richer game areas. Today, the persecution of this species continues unabated: in appearance it certainly lacks the aesthetic allure of the big cats with whom its shares much of its range, and it is likely to be added to the endangered list within the next decade.

Right: Apart from the gray wolf, the African wild dog is the most highly social of the canids. The largest of all the African canids, wild dogs hunt in packs and have a higher kill rate than the lions and leopards with whom they compete for food on the East African savanna.

WOLVES

Index

ACKNOWLEDGEMENTS

The publisher gratefully acknowledges the following agencies and photographers for supplying the photography for this book:

Alan Carey for front cover;
Philip Sharpe/RSPCA Photolibrary for pages 6-7, 98-99;
E A Janes/RSPCA Photolibrary for pages 8, 20-21, 30, 36 (left), 78-79, 88 (bottom), 94-95, 103, 108, 129;
Claudia Auer/RSPCA Photolibrary for pages 9, 130-131 (main);
Gunther Kopp/RSPCA Photolibrary for pages 10, 19, 24, 32, 40-41, 51, 56-57, 60-61, 67, 70 (left), 73, 75, 76-77, 80, 82-83, 86-87, 88 (top), 109, 110-111, back cover;
Andy Rouse for pages 11, 14 (top), 15 (top), 18, 22, 26, 28, 31, 34-35, 36-37 (main), 38 (bottom), 39, 42-43, 44 (both), 45, 48-49, 50, 64-65, 66, 68-69, 70-71, 72, 78 (left), 81, 85, 86 (left), 89, 90, 117, 118-119, 128, 135, 136-137;
Klaus-Peter Wolf/RSPCA Photolibrary for pages 12-13, 27, 91, 92-93;
Frank Krahmer/RSPCA Photolibrary for pages 14 (bottom), 25, 62-63, 96-97, 100-101, 102, 104, 112-113, 126-127, 132-133, 159;
Dr Matt Ruglys/RSPCA Photolibrary for pages 15 (bottom);
Mark Hamblin/RSPCA Photolibrary for pages 16-17, 52, 53, 55, 115;
David Langfield/RSPCA Photolibrary for page 23;
Stuart Harrop/RSPCA Photolibrary for page 29;
Colin Seddon/RSPCA Photolibrary for page 33;
William S Paton/RSPCA Photolibrary for pages 38 (top), 46-47;
Len Rue Jr for pages 58-59, 74, 106-107;
Birgit Koch/RSPCA Photolibrary for pages 84, 130 (left), 134;
Jonathan Plant/RSPCA Photolibrary for page 105;
Tim Martin/RSPCA Photolibrary for page 116;
Byron Jorjorian for pages 120, 121, 122, 123, 124-125;
John Downer/RSPCA Photolibrary for pages 138-139;
C Hamilton James/RSPCA Photolibrary for pages 142, 143, 144-145, 147;
Samantha Purdy/RSPCA Photolibrary for pages 148-149;
Robert Glover/RSPCA Photolibrary for page 151;
Richard Matthews/RSPCA Photolibrary for pages 152, 153;
Mike Lane/RSPCA Photolibrary for pages 155, 156-157.

WOLVES